THE QUEBEC ACT:
Protest and Policy

D1280964

CANADIAN HISTORICAL CONTROVERSIES

Series Editor
W. J. ECCLES

Department of History, University of Toronto

THE QUEBEC ACT:

Protest and Policy

HILDA NEATBY

Department of History
Queen's University, Kingston

p

PRENTICE-HALL ✦ OF CANADA, LTD.

h

Scarborough, Ontario

PRENTICE-HALL, INC., ENGLEWOOD CLIFFS, NEW JERSEY
PRENTICE-HALL INTERNATIONAL, INC., LONDON
PRENTICE-HALL OF AUSTRALIA, PTY., LTD., SYDNEY
PRENTICE-HALL OF INDIA, PVT., LTD., NEW DELHI
PRENTICE-HALL OF JAPAN, INC., TOKYO

Library of Congress Catalog Card No. 74-179445
0-13-748111-X-Pa
0-13-748129-2-Cl
1 2 3 4 5 76 75 74 73 72
PRINTED IN CANADA

Contents

Contents

Series Editor's Preface

The aim of this series is to compare and to subject to critical scrutiny, the ways in which historians have treated major issues in Canadian history. Each volume defines one issue in space and time, and indicates its importance for both the people concerned and later generations. Selected quotations from contemporary sources indicate the views of the people of the period; then, the historians' interpretations of the issue are given and discussed critically. Finally, the author indicates what needs to be done, pointing out, wherever possible, evidence not yet utilized or inadequately examined by earlier historians, and suggests new lines of approach that could place the issue in a more revealing light.

It is hoped that in this way the student of history will gain, not only a better understanding of the events, but also an insight into the way in which history is written. He will, it is hoped, become aware that there is no such thing as "definitive history," that the history of this country was not brought down the mountain engraved on ten stone tablets by certain eminent scholars whose opinions cannot be questioned. Events in a historian's own time influence the way in which he views the past, the questions he asks of it, the methods he employs in seeking the answers, and the values that govern his judgements. Thus, what the historian has written has continually to be subjected to critical examination and his interpretations qualified or revised.

If this series enables those interested in the history of Canada to approach it more critically, with a better appreciation of what has been done, and a clearer idea of what needs to be done, it will have served its purpose.

W. J. E.

THE QUEBEC ACT:
Protest and Policy

Introduction

A recent critic of Canadian education reports that school children complain bitterly of the series of "tidy little acts" pressed on their attention in the course of their study of the century following the cession of New France to Britain in 1763. If these "tidy little acts" are the enactments of 1774, 1791, 1840 and 1867, the complaint does indeed suggest that teachers and text books fail to do justice to the complexity of the problems which these statutes were designed to solve, or to the strenuous debates which generally preceded and followed them.

In this important group the Quebec Act holds a special place. It was the first Imperial statute to create a constitution for a British colony. This statute was passed at a great crisis in the affairs of the First Empire, and it has been seen by some as one cause of the American Revolution. It was destined to be cited as a precedent for similar enactments designed to suit the needs of the new kinds of colonies which composed the Second Empire. In some respects it even appears to embody the principles of the later Commonwealth. For all these reasons it has received special attention from historians of the British Empire. As it was also the first parliamentary statute to recognize the complexity of the relations between the two groups which together were to constitute the beginnings of the Canadian people, it has been considered a key piece of legislation by Canadian historians.

For all these reasons the Quebec Act has aroused much interest and much controversy. The purpose of this collection of papers is not so much to cast fresh light on the Act itself, as to offer it as an illustration of the way in which historical judgments are and must be made. Historians seek to reveal the truth. All good historians do reveal some truth. The particular truths they are able to show depend on time and circumstance, as well as on their own ability, diligence and good luck.

The commonest criticism of a historian, especially by the ill-informed, is that he is "biased." This word has been so overworked and abused that it is now freely applied (often with no supporting evidence) to any decided judgment favourable or unfavourable, on men or events. The word thus used has no meaning in historical criticism. Historical bias, it may be said, is caused by some current of emotion which carries man's reason off the straight line which should lead him to sound judgment based on adequate evidence; or perhaps to an admission that there is not sufficient evidence for a final judgment.

Obviously all historians are in danger of letting any strong personal opinions they may hold on religion, ethics, politics, or the social order prejudice their treatment of historical issues. All good historians are aware of this occupational hazard and try to guard against it. Less obviously, all historians are likely to be strongly influenced in their judgments by what may be generally considered right or wrong, expedient or otherwise, in their own age and society. It is easier to discount one's own personal views, and to give fair treatment to those of a dissenting contemporary, than to emancipate oneself from the whole climate of opinion in a given society, marking the subtle gradations from what may be accepted as eternal values at one extreme from purely temporary principles of expedience at the other. It may be very difficult for a historian so to emancipate himself from his surroundings as to give a fair judgment of what would have been right, wise or expedient in the very different times and circumstances of which he may be writing. It is his first obligation to be aware of the difficulty and to endeavour to overcome it. His success may well depend not only on his integrity and good will, but on the depth and the breadth of his scholarship.

The Quebec Act has been praised by some as a just and humane piece of legislation because it recognized the claim of the Canadians to be judged in certain matters by their own traditional laws and customs and to continue the practice of their own religion without being officially rated as second-class citizens. Also, by refraining from imposing or granting an elective assembly, it left them, for a time, governed by a generally benevolent oligarchy and relatively free from taxation.

Historians have differed in their opinions of this piece of legislation for a number of reasons. No one is willing to admit that he is opposed to humanity and justice. But conceptions of what is just and humane change with the times. If it is agreed that the historian must attempt to distinguish between his own conceptions of justice and those which prevailed in the times of which he writes, it must be admitted that not all historians dealing with the Quebec Act have stopped to ask themselves what men of ability and good will would have considered just in 1774. For example, would it have seemed right to them to establish the British state church, to contrive an adaptation of the Gallican church, to arrange some sort of compromise, or even to identify and imitate the American experiments at voluntarism? Many writers have passed a rapid and generally favourable judgment on the religious settlement of the Quebec Act. Very few have stated in detail what this settlement was. The possible alternatives have not always received impartial examination.

The moral judgment here has been further confused by a natural inclination to consider the morality and wisdom of the measure as partly determined by motive and therefore to try to deal with the motives of the authors of the Act. Some writers have suggested that these motives were not only mistaken but discreditable. Not all have been precise in distinguishing their judgment on the possible motives from their decision on the merit or otherwise of what was done.

A further complicating factor is that writers, especially Canadians, dealing with the Quebec Act may find their judgments on the motives and the policy of the Act blending with their conclusions about its effect on the subsequent history of Canada. They find it difficult not to ask themselves whether it would have been "better" for Quebec, and for the future Canada and North America, the Empire and the Commonwealth, to have tried or tried harder to bring about assimilation of Canadians to a possible or probable Anglo-Saxon majority. Would such assimilation have been possible? The views of the historians on this question are likely to depend very much on the time at which they write—that is, on the current views on nationalism, liberalism and democracy—to say nothing of current population trends.

There are other and more obvious reasons for the differing views of historians on the Quebec Act. Some who have written have not had access to, or have perhaps not troubled to use relevant source material, or, using it, have not fully grasped its significance. The Quebec Act presents a special difficulty here because in two important areas of investigation the evidence is wholly inadequate. It is difficult to determine what were the general views and wishes of the Canadian people in 1774. As most critics would agree that justice and humanity demanded at least some attention to the wishes of the Canadians, this gap in historical evidence is a serious one. Formal petitions by Canadians have survived. Some other evidence exists. Unfortunately, the majority of Canadians at that time could not write and it may be assumed that many things written have not survived or have not been found. Among the clergy, especially, many whose views would have been interesting may have thought it wiser not to express them in writing. It is difficult even today with the aid of scientific polls to say what, at a given moment, a given group of people "want." On the wants of Canadians in 1774, it is inevitable that the fragmentary evidence surviving should be interpreted in different ways.

Evidence is also inadequate on the views and motives of those who gave the Act its final form. The papers of Carleton, which would presumably have been invaluable, were not preserved. The Quebec Act seemed to carry out views which he had expressed during his stay in Canada (1766-1770) but almost nothing survives of comments and suggestions which he must have made during his stay in England in the years preceding the passing of the Act (1770-1774). Nor is there much other confidential material apart from a few memoranda and drafts of the Act which have been preserved in the Dartmouth papers. Here again historians, trying to discern some pattern where too many pieces are missing, are likely to come to different conclusions.

The following selection of primary materials presented as evidence on the situation in Canada preceding the Quebec Act and on the motives and policy which may have determined it, is of course arbitrary. The intention, however, has been to make the sampling as representative as possible. It is hoped that this collection will add to the reader's understanding and appreciation of the judgments of various historians on the Act itself which are discussed in Part 5 of this book.

PART 1

Some Evidence on the Genesis of the Act

On September 8, 1760, a year after the capture of Quebec, Vaudreuil, Governor of New France, surrendered the town of Montreal and the colony to the British commander, Jeffrey Amherst. The conditions of surrender, or articles of capitulation might be expected to have a bearing on British policy towards the conquered people. That they were indeed permanently binding was the view of Lord Mansfield.[1]

1. THE EXISTING CONSTITUTION AND LAWS

a. Articles of Capitulation, Montreal, September 8, 1760.[2]

ARTICLE XXVII
  The free exercise of the Catholic, Apostolic, and Roman Religion, shall subsist entire, in such manner that all . . . the people of the Towns and countries . . . shall continue to assemble . . . and to frequent the sacraments as heretofore, without being molested in any manner. . . . These people shall be obliged . . . to pay their Priests the tithes, and all the taxes they were used to pay under the Government of his most Christian Majesty.—"Granted, as to the free exercise of their religion, the obligation of paying the tithes to the Priests will depend on the King's pleasure."

ARTICLE XXX
  If by the treaty of peace, Canada should remain in the power of his Britannic Majesty, his most Christian Majesty shall continue to name the Bishop of the colony, who shall always be of the Roman communion, and under whose authority the people shall exercise the Roman Religion.—"Refused."

[Articles XXXI to XXXIII also relate to the Church requesting certain rights for the Bishop, which are referred back to the answer to

Article XXX, and also requesting complete protection for the Nuns to remain within their houses, to carry on their religious exercises and to be safe-guarded if necessary. These privileges were granted, but similar requests for the communities of men, that is, Jesuits and Recollets and the Sulpicians of Montreal, were "Refused till the King's pleasure be known."]

ARTICLE XXXVII

The Lords of the Manors, the Military and Civil officers, the Canadians as well in the Towns as in the country, the French settled, or trading, in the whole extent of the colony of Canada, and all other persons whatsoever, shall preserve the entire peaceable property and possession of the goods . . . [lands], merchandizes, furs and . . . even their ships. . . .—"Granted as in the XXVIth article."

b. The Treaty of Paris, February 10, 1763.[3]

The Treaty of Paris, a lengthy document establishing peace between Great Britain, France and Spain, refers briefly to the religious guarantees offered in the articles of capitulation. It does not refer to the property rights of Canadians remaining under British rule. The guarantee of freedom of worship in the Treaty is somewhat ambiguous;

. . . . His Britannick Majesty, on his side, agrees to grant the liberty of the Catholick religion to the inhabitants of Canada: he will, in consequence, give the most precise and most effectual orders, that his new Roman Catholic subjects may profess the worship of their religion according to the rites of the Romish church, as far as the laws of Great Britain permit . . .

c. The Royal Proclamation of 1763.[4]

On October 7, 1763, the government issued a Proclamation which, because of its significance in Canadian history, has come to be known as "The Proclamation of 1763." This instrument established civil government in the King's new possessions in North America. It is, however, couched in terms apparently so irrelevant to conditions in Quebec that one historian, C. W. Alvord, produced the ingenious theory that Quebec had been inserted as an afterthought, the Proclamation having been originally drawn without any intention of including Quebec with its special situation in the general arrangements.[5]

. . . [The Proclamation establishes four new governments, Quebec, East Florida, West Florida, and Grenada, and makes certain additions to the government of Nova Scotia and to the province of Georgia.] And whereas it will greatly contribute to the speedy settling our said new Governments, that our loving subjects should be informed of our Paternal care, for the security of the Liberties and Properties of those who are and shall become Inhabitants thereof, We have thought fit to publish and declare, by this Our Proclamation, that We have, in the Letters Patent under our Great Seal of Great Britain, by which the said Governments are constituted, given express Power and Direction to our Governors of our Said Colonies respectively, that so soon as the state and circumstances of the said Colonies will admit thereof, they shall, with the Advice and Consent of the Members of our Council, summon and call General Assemblies within the said Governments respectively . . . and We have also given Power to the said Governors, with the consent of our Said Councils, and the Representatives of the People . . . to make . . . Laws . . . for the Public Peace, Welfare, and good Government of our said Colonies . . . as near as may be agreeable to the Laws of England . . . and until such Assemblies can be called . . . all Persons Inhabiting in or resorting to our Said Colonies may confide in our Royal Protection for the Enjoyment of the Benefit of the Laws of our Realm of England; for which Purpose We have given Power . . . to the Governors of our said Colonies . . . to erect . . . with the Advice of our said Councils . . . Courts of Judicature . . . for hearing and determining all Causes, as well Criminal as Civil, according to Law and Equity, and as near as may be agreeable to the Laws of England, with Liberty to all Persons . . . in all Civil Cases, to appeal . . . to Us in our Privy Council.

d. The Lords of Trade to Egremont, June 8, 1763.[6]

That the King's advisors had been aware of the special situation in Quebec is shown by two documents produced in the summer of 1763 before the Proclamation was issued. The Lords of Trade, having been required to report to Lord Egremont, the minister responsible, on the management of the new possessions in North America, referred to the newly-acquired French colony in the following terms:

> It is obvious that the new Government of Canada . . . will . . . contain within it a very great number of French Inhabitants . . . and that the Number of such Inhabitants must greatly exceed, for a very long period of time, that of Your Majesty's . . . other Subjects who may attempt Settlements, even supposing the utmost Efforts of Industry on their part . . . in making new Settlements . . . From which Circumstances, it appears to Us that the Chief Objects of any new Form of Government to be erected in that Country ought to be to secure the ancient Inhabitants in all the Titles, Rights and Privileges granted to them by Treaty, and to increase as much as possible the Number of British and other new Protestant Settlers, which Objects We apprehend will be best obtain'd by the Appointment of a Governor and Council under Your Majesty's immediate Commission & Instructions. But the . . . particular Regulations and Provisions . . . will . . . come under Your Majesty's Consideration in the Draught of the Commission and Instructions to be prepared for each Governor . . .

e. Egremont to Governor James Murray, August 13, 1763.[7]

Egremont in writing to the new Governor, James Murray, also showed his awareness of a special situation, although his concern is chiefly with the effect of the religious concessions on security and foreign relations, rather than with laws of property.

> . . . His Majesty thinks it very material, that you should be apprized, that He has received Intelligence . . . that the French may be disposed to avail Themselves of the Liberty of the Catholick Religion granted to the Inhabitants of Canada, in order to keep up their Connection with France, and, by means of the Priests, to preserve such an Influence over the Canadians, as may induce them to join, whenever Opportunity should offer, in any attempts to recover that Country; It therefore becomes of the utmost Consequence to watch the Priests very narrowly, and to remove, as soon as possible, any of them, who shall attempt to go out of their sphere, and who shall busy themselves in any civil matters: For tho' the King has,

in the 4th Article of the Definitive Treaty, *agreed to grant the Liberty of the Catholick Religion to the Inhabitants of Canada*; and tho' His Majesty is far from entertaining the most distant thought of restraining *His new Roman Catholick Subjects from professing the Worship of their Religion according to the Rites of the Romish Church*: Yet the Condition, expressed in the same Article, must always be remembered, vizt: *As far as the Laws of Great Britain permit*, which Laws prohibit absolutely all Popish Hierarchy in any of the Dominions belonging to the Crown of Great Britain, and can only admit of a Toleration of the Exercise of that Religion . . . But, at the same Time, that I point out to you the necessity of adhering to [the laws of Great Britain] and of attending with the utmost Vigilance to the Behaviour of the Priests, the King relies on your acting with all proper Caution & Prudence in regard to a matter of so delicate a Nature as this of Religion; And that you will, as far as you can, consistently with your Duty in the Execution of the Laws, & with the Safety of the Country, avoid every Thing that can give the least unnecessary Alarm, or Disgust, to His Majesty's new Subjects.

f. Instructions to Governor Murray, December 7, 1763.[8]

Murray's official instructions, although they followed the general pattern of instructions to a colonial governor, permitted a temporary modification of the pattern laid down in the Proclamation of 1763. They confirmed the guarantees made on behalf of Canadians in the Treaty of Paris. They appeared, however, to assume that the general character of the colony in the future would be English and Protestant.

30. And it is Our further Will and Pleasure, that all . . . Inhabitants professing the Religion of the Romish Church, do . . . at such . . . Time . . . as You shall think proper, and in the Manner you shall think least alarming and inconvenient . . . deliver in upon Oath an exact Account of all Arms and Ammunition, of every Sort in their actual Possession . . .

31. You are as soon as possible to transmit to Us . . . an exact and particular Account of the . . . several Religious Communities of the Romish Church, their Rights, Claims Privileges and Property, and also the Number, Situation and Revenue of the several Churches . . . together with the Number of Priests or Curates officiating in such Churches.

32. You are not to admit of any Ecclesiastical Jurisdiction of the See of Rome, or any other foreign Ecclesiastical Jurisdiction whatsoever in the Province under your Government.

33. [Article 33 provides that the Church of England is to be established "both in Principles and Practice" and ultimately to be endowed with lands for maintaining both churches and schools.]

34. And You are to take especial Care, that God Almighty be devoutly and duly served throughout your Government, the Book of Common Prayer, as by Law established, read each Sunday and Holyday, and the blessed Sacrament administered according to the Rites of the Church of England.

35. You are not to prefer any Protestant Minister to any Ecclesiastical Benefice in the Province under Your Government, without a Certificate from the Right Reverend Father in God the Lord Bishop of London, of his being conformable to the Doctrine and Discipline of the Church of England, and of a good Life and Conversation; And if any Person hereafter preferred to a Benefice shall appear to you to give Scandal, either by his Doctrine or Manners, you are to use the best Means for his Removal.

g. Ordinance establishing civil courts, September 17, 1764.[9]

Governor Murray was in full agreement on the danger of Roman Catholicism, regarding Roman Catholics as politically unreliable. He was a decided "anglicizer" but not a harsh one. He was convinced that with time and patience the Canadians could be weaned from "religious error" and developed into an English colony. He therefore welcomed the Proclamation of October 7, 1763, accepting it as the policy of the government to attract English settlers in such numbers as would ultimately absorb the Canadians.

He was, however, aware of the immediate problem: that he must govern 65,000 Canadians whom he liked and wished to protect, and whose interests he thought were threatened by the few hundred English-speaking merchants and retailers who had given him some trouble.

Civil government was inaugurated on August 10, 1764. Murray then had to set up with the help of his Council a system of courts of justice, according to the English pattern. He did, however, take advantage of the wording of the Proclamation, "according to Law and Equity and as near as may be agreeable to the Laws of England," to make certain concessions to Canadian law and to Roman Catholics as citizens. Some thought these concessions over-generous; others found the ordinance cruelly unjust to Canadians. Murray was therefore freely criticized at the time and by his successor, Carleton. No one explained exactly what he ought to have done under the terms of the Proclamation.

Whereas it is highly expedient and necessary . . . that proper Courts of Judicature, with proper Powers and Authorities, and under proper Regulations, should be established and appointed:

His Excellency the Governor, by and with the Advice . . . of His Majesty's Council, and by Virtue of the Power and Authority to him given by His Majesty's Letters Patent, under the Great Seal of *Great Britain . . . Doth hereby Ordain and Declare,*

That a Superior Court of Judicature, or Court of King's Bench, be established in this Province . . .

In all Tryals in this Court, all His Majesty's Subjects in this Colony to be admitted on Juries without Distinction.

. . . That an inferior Court of Judicature, or Court of Common-Pleas, is hereby established, with Power and Authority, to determine all Property above the Value of *Ten Pounds* . . .

The Judges in this Court are to determine agreeable to Equity, having Regard nevertheless to the Laws of *England,* as far as the Circumstances and present Situation of Things will admit, until such Time as proper Ordinances for the Information of the People can be established by the Governor and Council, agreeable to the Laws of *England.*

The *French* Laws and Customs to be allowed and admitted in all Causes in this Court, between the Natives of this Province, where the Cause of Action arose before the first Day of October, One Thousand Seven Hundred and Sixty-four . . .

Canadian Advocats, Proctors, &c. may practise in this Court.

It will be noticed that the ordinance apparently allowed Roman Catholics to serve on juries in the King's Bench and to practise as lawyers in the Common Pleas. It seems likely that they sat on juries in both courts, something Roman Catholics in England could not do. There is also evidence that in the Court of Common Pleas, even though the ordinance limited the use of Canadian law and custom to suits originating before October 1, 1764, this law was in practice employed in all Canadian cases in the Common Pleas where it seemed equitable, the court becoming known as "the Canadian Court."

2. CONTROVERSY IN QUEBEC OVER THE LAWS AND THE FORM OF GOVERNMENT

a. Presentments of the Grand Jury, October 16, 1764.[10]

Murray's ordinance sparked a prolonged and bitter controversy which was not settled until the passing of the Quebec Act. English merchants in the province were alarmed at concessions made to Canadian Roman Catholics. They took advantage of the right of the Grand Jury to make representations to the authorities on any matter thought to be of importance for the peace and good government of the community to include in the presentments of the Grand Jury, summoned as a preliminary to the Quarter Sessions in the District of Quebec in the fall of 1764, a number of criticisms of the ordinance. These were signed by English and Canadians alike. To these presentments, however, the English members added several other articles signed by themselves alone.

. . . . Among the many grievances which require redress this seems not to be the least, that persons professing the Religion of the Church of Rome do acknowledge the supremacy and jurisdiction of the Pope . . . have been [empannelled], [in] Grand and petty Jurys even where Two protestants were partys, and whereas the Grand Inquest of a County City or Borough of the Realm of Great Britain, are obliged by their Oath to present to a Court of Quarter Sessions or assises, what even appears an open violation of the Laws and Statutes of the Realm. . . . We therefore believe nothing can be more dangerous . . . than admitting such persons to be sworn on Jurys, who by the Laws are disabled from holding any Office Trust or Power, more especially in a Judicial Capacity . . .

That. By the Definitive Treaty the Roman Religion was only tolerated in the province of Quebec so far as the Laws of Great Britain admit, it was and is enacted by the 3^d Jam^s 1st Chap^r 5th Section 8th no papist or popish Recusant Convict, shall practice "the Common Law, as a Councellor, Clerk, Attorney, or Sollicitor nor shall practice the Civil Law, as Advocate or proctor. . . ." We therefore believe that the admitting persons of the Roman Religion, who own the authority, supremacy and jurisdiction [of] the Church of Rome, as Jurors, is an open Violation of our most sacred Laws and Libertys, and tending to the utter subversion of the protestant Religion and his Majesty's power authority, right, and possession of the province to which we belong.

b. Statement of English Jurors (undated).[11]

The signers of the presentments, vigorously attacked by Murray as "licentious Fanaticks," later (from the evidence of the following document) offered an explanation which appears to be very like a retraction of a claim which on second thoughts may have seemed to some of them harsh and intolerant.

As the presentment made by the protestant members of the Jury, wherein the impannelling of Roman Catholicks upon Grand petty Juries, even where two protestants are the parties, is complained of. As this very presentment has been openly & ungenerously used as a handle to set his Majesty's old & new Subjects at varience in this province, we cannot help endeavour^g to set the public right in this particular in which they have been so grossly imposed on: What gave birth to this presentmt. was the following short, but pithy Paragraph, in the Ordinance of the 17th Day of Septr last.

"In all Tryalls in this Court all his Majesty's Subjects in this Colony to be admitted on Juries without any distinction:" This is qualifying the whole province at once for an Office which the best & most sensible people in it are hardly able to discharge: It then occur'd to the Jury that was laying a Subjects life, liberty & property too open, & that both old & new Subjects might be apprehensive of the consequence from the unlimited admission of Jurymen His Majesty's lately acquired Subjects cannot take it amiss, that his ancient subjects remonstrate ag^t this practice as being contrary to the laws of the realm of England, the benefit of which they think they have a right to, nor ought it to give offence when they demand that a protestant Jury should be impannelled when the litigating parties are protestants such were the real motives of the Presentment, and we can aver that nothing further was meant by the quotation from the Statute.

That the subscribers of the presentment meant to remove every Roman Catholick from holding any office or filling any public employment is to all intents and purposes a most vile groundless insinuation & utterly inconsistent: Sentiments & intentions such as these we abhor, & are only sorry that principles do not allow us to admit Roman Catholicks as Jurors upon a cause betwixt two protestants; perhaps theirs hold us in the same light in a Case betwixt two Catholicks, and we are very far from finding fault with them, the same liberty that we take of thinking for ourselves we must freely indulge to others.

c. Statement by French Members of the Grand Jury, October 26, 1764.[12]

Meanwhile the Canadian members of the Grand Jury, having learned of the additional presentment by their colleagues, issued their own statement. Not only did they repudiate the articles that they had signed, along with the English Canadians, on the ground that they had not fully understood what they had signed and therefore were not responsible for the criticism of the ordinance which had angered Murray; they concluded with a special statement against the articles signed by the English jurors only, suggesting that Canadians should not serve as jurors. They point out,

That H. M[ty] being informed that all the Subjects forming this Province were Catholics still believed them capable as such of taking the Oath of Loyalty, and therefore fit to be admitted to the service of their Country, in such a way as they shall be thought qualified for. It would be shameful to believe that the Canadians, New Subjects, cannot serve their King either as Serjeant, or Officers, it would be a most humiliating thought, and very discouraging to free Subjects who have been admitted to the Privileges of the Nation, and their Rights, as explained by H.M. For more than six Months we have had Catholic Canadian Officers in the Upper Country, and a Number of Volunteers aiding to repulse the Enemies of the Nation; and cannot a man who exposes himself freely to shed his blood in the Service of his King and of the Nation be admitted to positions where he can serve the Nation and the Public as a Juror, since he is a subject? The 3rd of James I. Chap. 5, Sec. 8, only refers to Catholics who may enter the Kingdom, and as there has never been any law in any Kingdom without some exception [something seems to have been omitted from the original but the sense seems to be that they are confident that England will ultimately admit them even as Catholics to national rights and that the law cannot be intended to "seek to make them slaves"].

d. Murray to the Board of Trade, October 29, 1764.[13]

Murray, angered by the criticisms of the Grand Jury and now probably aware, as he may not have been before, that even a gradual introduction of English law would work a hardship on Canadians, and that his own well-meant ordinance was not an adequate compromise, wrote home pleading for consideration for them although perhaps without any very clear idea of what could be done.

Little, very little, will content the New Subjects but nothing will satisfy the Licentious Fanaticks Trading here, but the expulsion of the Canadians who are perhaps the bravest and the best race upon the Globe, a Race who cou'd they be indulged with a few priveledges wch the Laws of England deny to Roman Catholicks at home, wou'd soon get the better of every National Antipathy to their Conquerors and become the most faithful and most useful set of Men in this American Empire.

I flatter myself there will be some Remedy found out even in the Laws for the Relief of this People, if so, I am positive the popular clamours in England will not prevent the Human Heart of the King from following its own Dictates. I am confident too my Royal Master will not blame the unanimous opinion of his Council here for the Ordonnance establishing the Courts of Justice, as nothing less cou'd be done to prevent great numbers from emigrating directly, and certain I am, unless the Canadians are admitted on Jurys, and are allowed Judges and Lawyers who understand their Language his Majesty will lose the greatest part of this Valuable people.

The closing words of this extract indicate a fear that appeared in more than one despatch of Murray's, that the province built up by the French with such care might even become depopulated. Present knowledge of the situation of most Canadians makes the idea appear entirely unrealistic. Few could have afforded to go to France, and other English colonies would have been even less desirable. It may be that Canadians, naturally desirous of exacting reasonable concessions from Great Britain, suggested and encouraged Murray's fear.[14]

e. Address of French Citizens, January 7, 1765.[15]

Upwards of one hundred Canadians sent a formal petition to the King praising Murray and his ordinance and asking for freedom from discrimination on religious grounds, and for the right to have their causes heard in their own language.

. . . . We have during the past four years, enjoyed the Beneficence of the Government, and we should still enjoy it, if Messrs the English Jurors were as submissive to the wise decisions of the Governor and his Council, as we are; if they were not seeking by new regulations, by the introduction of which they hope to make us their slaves, to change at once the order and administration of Justice, if they were not desirous of making us argue our Family Rights in a foreign tongue, and thereby depriving us of those Persons, who from their knowledge of our Customs, can understand us, settle our differences, and administer Justice at slight expense . . .

We entreat Your Majesty with the deepest and most respectful submission to confirm the system of Justice which has been established for the French, by the deliberations of the Governor and Council . . . to permit us to transact our Family Affairs in our own tongue, to follow our customs, in so far as they are not opposed to the general Wellbeing of the Colony, and to grant that a Law may be published in our Language . . .

This petition suggests first that Murray's ordinance had been very generously interpreted so that the court of Common Pleas had become a kind of Canadian Court; and second that the English jurors questioning the right of French notaries to practise and French jurors to act was not unnaturally seen as a threat to their freedom to use the French language in legal matters.

3. COMMENTS ON THE OPERATION OF THE LAWS: BRITAIN

a. Opinion of Attorney and Solicitor General on Status of Roman Catholics, June 10, 1765.[16]

Meanwhile the various reports on the state of Quebec had caused concern in London. An order from the Board of Trade to the law officers to report on the legal status of Roman Catholics in the new possessions elicited a brief and unambiguous reply.

We . . . are humbly of Opinion, that His Majesty's Roman Catholick Subjects residing in the Countries, ceded to His Majesty in America, by the Definitive Treaty of Paris, are not subject, in those Colonies, to the Incapacities, disabilities, and Penalties, to which Roman Catholicks in this Kingdom are subject by the Laws thereof. [FLr. NORTON, Wm. DE GREY]

b. Report of Attorney and Solicitor General, April 4, 1766.[17]

Less than a year later a detailed report from the law officers condemned Murray's ordinance and its application in the Province of

Quebec, implying that Canadian laws should not have been disturbed and making practical recommendations for the future.

> There is not a *Maxim* of the *Common Law* more certain than that a Conquer'd people retain their ancient Customs till the Conqueror shall declare New Laws. To change at once the Laws and manners of a settled Country must be attended with hardship and Violence; and therefore wise Conquerors having provided for the security of their Dominion, proceed gently and indulge their Conquere'd subjects in all local Customs which are in their own nature indifferent, and which have been received as rules of property or have obtained the force of Laws, It is the more material that this policy be persued in *Canada*; because it is a great and antient Colony long settled and much Cultivated, by French Subjects, who now inhabit it to the number of Eighty or one hundred thousand.

They therefore recommend that in commercial cases and actions for personal damages the judges bear in mind that "the substantial *maxims* of Law and Justice are every where the same" and that they act accordingly. They suggest that laws relating to real property be unchanged, the Canadian law being continued. They recommend the use of English criminal law as being a particularly beneficial part of the English constitution.

> This Certainty and this Lenity are the *Benefits* intended by his Majesty's Royal proclamation, so far as concerns Judicature. *These* are *Irrevocably* Granted and ought to be secured to his Canadian subjects, according to his Royal Word. For this purpose it may not be improper upon the appointment of a new Govr. with a *new Commission* revised and Consider'd by your Lordships, to direct that Governor to publish an explanatory proclamation in the Province, to quiet the minds of the People as to the true meaning of the Royal proclamation of Oct[r] 1763 in Respect to their local Customs and usages, more especially in Titles of Land and Cases of Real property.

c. Draft of Instructions to the Governor of Quebec, June 1766.[18]

Following these generally liberal recommendations instructions were prepared in June 1766 informing the Governor in Quebec that the ordinances on the courts of justice were repealed and that new ones were to be passed. In future, Canadians were to serve as jurors and as legal counsel in all courts and also as justices of the peace. The recommendations of the law officers on substantive law were to be followed, using the Canadian land law and English criminal law. The instructions conclude:

> And whereas it was, from a just sense of the lenity and certainty of the administration of justice in this kingdom in matters affecting the life and liberty of the subject, that we were induced to extend to our Canadian subjects by our royal Proclamation of the 7 of October 1763, the benefits of this constitution, not intending thereby to abrogate the laws and customs of Canada in matters of tenure, or the succession and alienation of real and personal estates; IT IS THEREFORE OUR WILL AND PLEASURE, that you do, as soon as conveniently may be, issue a proclamation in our name, explanatory of this our royal intention, in order to quiet the minds of our good subjects in respect of their local customs and usages, more especially in titles to land and cases of real property.
>
> And whereas it will be highly necessary and expedient, that the rules of process and the practice of the courts herein before directed to be established should be ascertained and promulged by proper authority; IT IS THEREFORE OUR WILL AND PLEASURE, that the chief justice of our said province do, with the assistance of the other judges, and of the attorney general of our Province of Quebec [prepare] a plan for this purpose . . . seriously reflecting of how great importance it is, that the forms of proceeding should be as simple, easy and summary, as may consist with the advancement of right, and the protection of innocence; AND . . . when the said plan shall have been so formed . . . it be enacted into a law by an ordinance of our governor and council, and such ordinance transmitted to us in the accustomed manner for our royal approbation.

d. Fowler Walker to Lord Dartmouth, October 17, 1765.[19]

The instructions of June 1766, which might have reached Quebec as Lt.-Gov. Carleton, acting for Murray, began his administration in the fall of 1766, were not sent. This was partly because of political rivalries unconnected with Quebec. There was, however, another and a valid reason. Already doubts were being privately raised about the government of Quebec which went far beyond criticisms of policy. In the fall of 1765 Fowler Walker, a member of Lincoln's Inn, appointed by the merchants as their agent in London, addressed to Lord Dartmouth a letter questioning the right of Governor and Council to legislate for Quebec, in view of the fact that the Proclamation of October 7, 1763, had promised an Assembly, and that Murray's public commission authorized government by Assembly only.

The proposition, which I would with the greatest deference submit to the consideration of his Majesty's Ministers, is, that the Governor and Council of Quebec, are not invested with any legal authority, "to ordain laws and ordonnances for the public peace and welfare and good Government of the province" notwithstanding they have taken upon themselves to do so.

Should this proposition be found to be true, the immediate necessity of forming a legislative body in so populous a province, is a point of so important a nature, that I am well assured it will be duly attended to—But if on the contrary, his Majesty's ministers should be of opinion, that a full legislative power is already vested in the Governor and Council, I am afraid, a conclusion of a very disagreeable nature will necessarily follow.

I am very sensible my Lord, that his Majesty . . . had by his royal prerogative, an undoubted right, to place the legislative power in that Country, in the Governor and Council solely, without giving the people any share therein . . . but what I beg leave to contend, is, that his Majesty by a solemn Act, namely his letters patent . . . and consequently, previous and antecedent, to any instructions given to the governor thereof, having thought proper to declare, that the power of ordaining laws, should be jointly placed in the Governor, with the consent of his Majesty's Council, viz., *the representatives of the people,* has thereby abrig'd himself, of the power of exercising his prerogative (consistently with his dignity) in a different manner . . . by any subsequent act . . .

e. Lord Mansfield in Campbell v. Hall, 1774.[20]

Fowler Walker's opinion was later confirmed by Lord Mansfield's judgment in Campbell v. Hall, already referred to. The judgment referred to a case in Grenada (like Quebec constituted under the Proclamation of 1763). Lord Mansfield declared invalid duties levied in Grenada, by royal proclamation, after October 1763 on the ground that, by the Proclamation of October 7, 1763, the King had vested the power which he did possess over a conquered people in a future elected assembly.

"You will observe in the Proclamation there is no legislation reserved to be exercised by the King, or by the governor and council under his authority, or in any other method or manner until the assembly should be called: the promise imports the contrary.
. . . We therefore think that . . . the King had immediately and irrevocably granted to all who were or should become inhabitants . . . that the subordinate legislation over the island should be exercised by an assembly with the consent of governor and council, in like manner as in the other provinces under the King."

4. PROPOSALS FOR A NEW CONSTITUTION

a. Petition of Quebec Traders [1764?].[21]

While the various comments on the constitution were being made, suggestions for a new and better system were being presented and considered. The first came from the English-Speaking merchants and traders in Quebec in the form of a petition, probably in 1764. Having made a number of complaints about the character of the military government, their sufferings from the interruption to trade caused by Pontiac's Rising and complaints about Murray's "vexatious, oppressive, unconstitutional" ordinances, they continue,

Your Petitioners . . . most humbly pray your Majesty . . . to appoint a Governor over us, acquainted with other maxims of Government than Military only; And . . . to order a House of Representatives to be chosen in this as in other your Majesty's Provinces; there being a number more than Sufficient of Loyal and well affected Protestants, exclusive of military Officers, to form a competent and respectable House of Assembly; and your Majesty's new Subjects, if your Majesty shall think fit, may be allowed to elect Protestants without burdening them with such Oaths as in their present mode of thinking they cannot conscientiously take.

b. Petition of the London Merchants, 1764.[22]

The London merchants forwarded the petition assuring His Majesty of the truth "of the several Allegations contained in the Address" and petitioning,

> That the Government of those your Majesty's Dominions may be at least put upon the same footing with the rest of your Majesty's American Colonies or upon any other footing that may be thought Essential for the preservation of the Lives Liberties and Properties of all your Majesty's most faithfull Subjects as well as for the increase and support of the Infant Commerce to and from that Part of the World.

c. Carleton to Shelburne, Nov. 25, Dec. 24, 1767; Jan. 20, 1768.[23]

Murray was called back to England in the spring of 1766. His successor, Lieutenant-Governor Carleton, having been made fully aware of the various comments on and complaints about the system of Quebec, came out prepared to consider the situation and to make recommendations for a change. During his administration Carleton was instructed, with the help of his law officers, to prepare a report on the defects of the legal system and to make recommendations for a remedy. Carleton found himself in disagreement with his law officers, Chief Justice William Hey and Attorney-General Francis Maseres, who were not in favour of a wholesale revival of pre-conquest Canadian civil law. There was general agreement, however, that Canadians must retain the laws governing the ownership and transfer of real property. Roughly three plans were considered: a special code combining Canadian and English law; a general basis of English law with the specific introduction of necessary Canadian laws; a revival of Canadian law with specific introduction of some English laws.

Carleton's letters, which follow, although not in the order in which they were written, consider the situation in the province, the problem of the law and the question of an Assembly. These letters are an important source of information on the situation in Quebec but, as historical evidence, they must be weighed and valued in the light of the other available evidence.

On December 24th, 1767 Carleton wrote a letter containing the substance of his reflections on the legal problem and the best solution of it.

To conceive the true State of the People of this Province . . . 'tis necessary to recollect, they are not a Migration of Britons, who brought with them the Laws of England, but a Populous and long established Colony, reduced by the King's Arms, to submit to His Dominion, on *certain Conditions*: That their Laws and Customs were widely Different from those of England, but founded on natural Justice and Equity, as well as these . . .

This System of Laws established Subordination, from the first to the lowest, which preserved the internal Harmony, they enjoyed untill our Arrival, and secured Obedience to the Supreme Seat of Government from a very distant Province. All this Arrangement, in one Hour, We overturned, by the Ordinance of the Seventeenth of September One Thousand seven hundred and sixty four, and Laws, ill adapted to the Genius of the Canadians, to the situation of the Province, and to the Interests of Great Britain, unknown, and unpublished were introduced in their Stead; A Sort of Severity, if I remember right, never before practiced by any Conqueror, even where the People, without Capitulation, submitted to His Will and Discretion.

How far this Change of Laws, which Deprives such Numbers of their Honors, Privileges, Profits, and Property, is conformable to the Capitulation of Montreal, and Treaty of Paris; How far this Ordinance, which affects the Life, Limb, Liberty, and Property of the Subject, is within the Limits of the Power, His Majesty has been pleased to Grant to the Governor and Council; How far this Ordinance, which in a Summary Way, Declares the Supreme Court of Judicature shall Judge all Cases Civil and Criminal by Laws unknown and unpublished to the People, is agreeable to the natural Rights of Mankind, I humbly submit; This much is certain, that it cannot long remain in Force, without a General Confusion and Discontent— . . .

The most advisable Method, in my Opinion, for removing the present, as well as for preventing future Evils, is to repeal that Ordinance [of 17th Sept. 1764] . . . and for the present leave the Canadian Laws almost entire; such Alterations might be afterwards made in them . . . so as to reduce them to that System, His Majesty should think fit, without risking the Dangers of too much Precipitation; or else; such Alterations might be made in the old and those new Laws Judged necessary to be immediately introduced, and publish the whole as a Canadian Code, as was practised by Edward the First after the Conquest of Wales—

An important question that Carleton had to consider was the form of government to be established in the province should the English petition for an elected Assembly according to the promise of the Proclamation of 1763 be granted. In his letter of November 25th, 1767, he gives a sketch of the situation in Quebec which has often been quoted and which helps to explain why he was inclined to reject the usual model of government for an English colony.

Having arrayed the Strength of His Majesty's old and new Subjects, and shewn the great Superiority of the Latter, it may not be amiss to observe, that there is not the least Probability, this present Superiority should ever diminish, on the Contrary 'tis more than probable it will increase and strengthen daily: The Europeans, who migrate never will prefer the long unhospitable Winters of Canada, to the more chearful Climates, and more fruitful Soil of his Majesty's Southern Provinces; The few old Subjects at present in this Province, have been mostly left here by Accident, and are either disbanded Officers, Soldiers, or Followers of the Army, who, not knowing how to dispose of themselves elsewhere, settled where they were left at the Reduction; or else they are Adventurers in Trade, or such as could not remain at Home, who set out to mend their Fortunes, at the opening of this new Channel for Commerce, but Experience has taught almost all of them, that this Trade requires a Strict Frugality, they are Strangers to, or to which they will not submit; so that some, from more advantagious Views elsewhere, others from Necessity, have already left this Province, and I greatly fear many more, for the same Reasons, will follow their Example in a few Years; But while this severe Climate, and the Poverty of the Country discourages all but the Natives, it's Healthfulness is such, that these multiply daily, so that, barring Catastrophe shocking to think of, this Country must, to the end of Time, be peopled by the Canadian Race, who already have taken such firm Root, and got to so great a Height, that any new Stock transplanted will be totally hid, and imperceptible amongst them, except in the Towns of Quebec and Montreal.

However, Carleton was not much in favour of colonial assemblies anywhere in America as may be seen from his letter of January 20th, 1768.[24]

... the better Sort of Canadians fear nothing more than popular Assemblies, which, they conceive, tend only to render the People refractory and insolent; Enquiring what they thought of them, they said, they understood some of our Colonies had fallen under the King's Displeasure, owing to the Misconduct of their Assemblies, and that they should think themselves unhappy, if a like Misfortune befell them. It may not be improper here to observe, that the British Form of Government, transplanted into this Continent, never will produce the same Fruits as at Home, chiefly, because it is impossible for the Dignity of the Throne, or Peerage to be represented in the American Forests; Besides, the Governor having little or nothing to give away, can have but little Influence; in Place of that, as it is his Duty to retain all in proper Subordination, and to restrain those Officers, who live by Fees, from running them up to Extortion; these Gentlemen, put into Offices, that require Integrity, Knowledge and Abilities, because they bid the highest Rent to the Patentee, finding themselves checked in their Views of Profit, are disposed to look on the Person, who disappoints them, as their Enemy, and without going so far as to forfeit their Employments, they in general will be shy of granting that Assistance, the King's Service may require, unless they are all equally disinterested or equally Corrupt. It therefore follows, where the executive Power is lodged with a Person of no Influence, but coldly assisted by the rest in Office, and where the two first Branches of the Legislature have neither Influence, nor Dignity, except it be from the extraordinary Characters of the Men, That a popular Assembly, which preserves it's full Vigor, and in a Country where all Men appear nearly upon a Level, must give a strong Bias to Republican Principles; Whether the independent Spirit of a Democracy is well adapted to a subordinate Government of the British Monarchy, or their uncontrolable Notions ought to be encouraged in a Province, so lately Conquered, and Circumstanced as this is, I with great Humility submit to the Superior Wisdom of His Majesty's Councils: for my own part, I shall think myself Fortunate, If I have succeeded in rendering clear Objects, not allways distinctly discernable at so great a Distance . . .

d. Board of Trade to the Privy Council, July 10, 1769.[25]

Meanwhile the Board of Trade, in spite of Carleton's warnings, had been trying to devise a plan for an Assembly suited to conditions in the province of Quebec. The scheme they devised would have allowed Roman Catholics to sit and vote as members, but the electoral districts were so arranged that Protestants must always have a majority of at least one in the House. This result was achieved by exempting members from rural districts, and them only, from the oath of the Test Act against transubstantiation. This meant that the members from the towns would be English, presumably English merchants, who would, however, be balanced by the Canadian rural members who were expected to be of the seigneurial class. The Board emphasized that they were suggesting an experiment and that changes in the future must be expected.

> With regard to the House of Representatives . . . it will, we presume, be neither practicable nor expedient, in the present state of that Colony, to give it such a shape and form, as shall be considered to be fixed and permanent under all circumstances; every establishment of this nature must be considered merely in the light of experiment, so far at least as depends upon the form in which it shall be first convened, open in all cases that regard the places which are to elect Representatives, the number to be elected, and the form of their qualifications, and proceedings, to such alterations, as a Variation in the state and circumstances of the Colony shall from time to time require . . .

In the same report, the Board of Trade dealt with the question of the status of the Roman Catholic Church. They referred to promises made in the Articles of Capitulation and in the Treaty of Paris in 1763. They differed both from Attorney-General Marriott and from Lord Chief Justice Mansfield in that they regarded the Treaty as superseding any promises made in the capitulation, the articles of which, therefore, they stated were no longer binding.

> . . . the Capitulation is now, we apprehend, out of the question, and the whole depends upon the fourth Article of the Treaty of Paris, which contains nothing more in respect to the Religion of the Church of Rome, than barely a free exercise of it by the new Subjects, so far as the Laws of England permit.
>
> Under these circumstances . . . it ought to be recommended . . . [They recommend abolition of the Jesuits and of the Chapter of Quebec, prohibition of any more admissions to the Recollets or to the women's orders, the combining of the Seminaries of Quebec and Montreal under one Superior, in order to train a limited number of

priests] . . . That, as being necessary to the due execution of the Treaty of Paris, a proper person be licensed by His Majesty, during Pleasure, to Superintend the affairs of the Romish Church; but it will be essential to the legality of such appointment, that the powers should be so limited and circumscribed, as that it may not violate or impeach His Majesty's Supremacy in all causes, as well Ecclesiastical as Civil . . .[26]

e. Petition of English Merchants (Quebec) [1770?].[27]

That your Majesty's British Subjects residing in this Province have set examples and given every encouragement in their power to promote Industry, are the principal Importers of British Manufactures, carry on three fourths of the Trade of this Country, annually return a considerable Revenue into Your Majesty's Exchequer in Great Britain; and though the great advantages this Country is naturally capable of are many and obvious for promoting the Trade and Manufactures of the Mother Country, yet for some time past, both its Landed and Commercial Interests have been declining, and if a General Assembly is not soon order'd by Your Majesty to make and enforce due obedience to Laws for encouraging Agriculture, regulating the Trade, discouraging such Importations from the other Colonies as impoverish the Province, Your Petitioners have the greatest reason to apprehend their own ruin as well as that of the Province in general.

f. Petition of Canadians [1770].[28]

The Canadians, as it appears from internal evidence, entrusted to Carleton who returned to Britain in 1770 what seems to have been their first entirely unambiguous demand for a total restoration, or recognition, of their Laws.

From the Moment, Sire, of the union of this Province to the Dominion of your Crown, your most humble servants have taken the Liberty of frequently representing to you, of what importance to their interests it was to be judged and governed according to the Laws Customs and regulations under which they were born, which serve as the Basis and Foundation of their possessions, and are the rule of their families, and how painful and at the same time how humiliating it has been to them to be excluded from the offices which they might fill in this Province, for the Service of Your Majesty, and the Comfort of Your Canadian People,—the only way to excite emulation . . . [They conclude by stating their conviction that their religion cannot possibly be a reason for excluding them from the Monarch's "favours," meaning, presumably, their appointement to public office.]

g. Opinions of the Law Officers 1772-3.

Carleton left Quebec to go to London in 1770 and remained there until after the passage of the Quebec Act in 1774. During this period the British government added to the reports of Carleton and of the Chief Justice, Hey, and the Attorney-General, Maseres, of Quebec reports in Britain from Solicitor General Wedderburn, Attorney General Thurlow, and Advocate General Marriott. These reports, differing in detail, generally agreed on the difficulty of calling an assembly. All agreed on the need for preserving some Canadian law. Wedderburn suggested

> That the Laws & Usages touching the Tenure, Descent & Alienation of Land or real Property, and the Distribution of the Goods of such of His Majesty's Canadian Subjects as shall die intestate, which were in force on the 13th of Septr 1759, shall be observed and maintained in all Questions that shall arise concerning the same in any of the Courts of Justice in the Province of Quebec, except in such cases as are hereafter declared.[29]

Wedderburn recommended, however, that this clause should not extend to lands granted in "free & common Soccage" and that any inhabitant of the province over the age of 25 years be allowed to convert his holdings from seigneurial to freehold tenure. Attorney General Edward Thurlow took a somewhat different view.

> The Canadians seem to have been strictly entitled by the *jus gentium* to their property, as they possessed it upon the capitulation and treaty of peace, together with all its qualities and incidents, by tenure or otherwise, and also to their personal liberty; for both which they were to expect your Majesty's gracious protection.

It seems a necessary consequence that all those laws by which that property was created, defined, and secured must be continued to them . . .

. . . It is easy to imagine what infinite disturbance it would create to introduce new and unknown measures of justice; doubt and uncertainty in the transaction; disappointment and loss in consequence.

The same kind of observation applies with still greater force against a change of the criminal law, in proportion as the examples are more striking, and the consequences more important . . .

. . . new subjects, acquired by conquest, have a right to expect from the benignity and justice of their conqueror the continuation of all these old laws, and they seem to have no less reason to expect it from his wisdom . . . He seems . . . to provide better for the public peace and order, by leaving them in the habit of obedience to their accustomed laws than by undertaking the harsher task of compelling a new obedience to laws unheard of before . . .[30]

Advocate General Marriott, on the other hand, agreed with Wedderburn. Canadians needed only complete assurance of their property laws.

It would probably answer every just and reasonable purpose, and would tend perfectly to quiet the minds of your Majesty's Canadian subjects, if a bill were to pass in parliament to the following effect. That in all cases of wills, tenures, ancient rents, quit-rents, service not being military, divisions of lands, and transfers, hypothecations, or charges and pledges, or incumbrances of property, moveable and immoveable, and of hereditary descent, or partition of dower, or distribution in cases of intestacy, the legitime, or portion of children and widows, and of all deeds, leases, and contracts, the ancient laws, customs, and usages of Canada shall be valid.[31]

h. Opinion of "Canadiens Vrais Patriotes" July 14, 1773.[32]

Toward the end of 1773 English and Canadians each sent in final petitions, the English asking an Assembly and the Canadians their "ancient laws, privileges, and customs," and both asking that the province be extended to its former boundaries. The copy of one petition which was perhaps not sent has been found in a private collection and is significant as suggesting that the unanimity of Canadians was less clear-cut than the public papers suggest. It is signed only "Les Canadiens Vrais Patriotes."

 . . . It is intended as we are told to leave to this Province its local laws of property, thus by giving a reasonable interpretation to the Proclamation, as is just . . . because by the 37th article of the General Capitulation of all Canada General Amherst promised to the Canadians . . . the entire peaceable property and possession of their goods. . . . If the entire peaceable property and possession of their goods is solemnly promised is it possible to change or to suppress or abolish the laws by which these goods are governed since without these Laws we cannot enjoy them as they should be enjoyed and as they always have been enjoyed? . . . But [the Minister] wishes . . . contrary to the promises made to the Canadians by the royal Proclamation that they should enjoy along with all British subjects the benefits and advantages of English laws, to deprive them of these in giving to the Governor with the Council, without the aid of the House of Assembly, complete legislative power . . . complete right (without consulting the people and their true interests) to change, alter, reform, and even abolish their ancient laws of property following his caprice and his will, and to impose on them all such taxes as he may judge proper. Such a power cannot be granted to a Governor and Council without derogating entirely from the prudent and wise constitution of the British Government. His Most Excellent Majesty and the honourable Parliament . . . no doubt will refuse to accept such a plan which would only tend to the extinction of our personal rights, which His Most Excellent Majesty by his Proclamation has promised that we should enjoy as British subjects and assuring us that we should profit entirely from the benefit of English laws of which this part is one of the principal advantages which is granted and promised by the said Proclamation. If it is not possible according to the British Constitution to establish in this Province a House of Assembly into which Canadians of the Gallican Church should be admitted we cannot reasonably consent to the establishment of one from which they must be excluded . . .
Our laws of property granted to us we consent that the Governor with an adequate Council may have . . . power to make laws solely on police matters conformably to the former usages . . . provided

... that this power should not ... alter ... the basic laws concerning property in the smallest detail. Nor are we opposed to the granting of the right to anyone to renounce for himself and his family local laws of the province in matters of marriage, dowry and inheritance ... to fulfill the promise of His Most Gracious Majesty that we should enjoy the benefit and the advantages of English law and to give every satisfaction to the old subjects who are already established here and to those who may come and settle here in the future. There is not the least difficulty in the laws of England being followed in this province in matters of admiralty and in commercial matters since these do not concern real property [*propriété*].

The inhabitants of this province cannot reasonably oppose the establishment of a House of Assembly if it is composed as it should be of old and new subjects without distinction. ... The irreproachable conduct that [the Canadians] have followed since the Conquest, their submission to the British Government, should be a sure guarantee to the Mother Country that they will not abuse any alteration in its ancient laws that may be made in their favour. His Most Excellent Majesty by assuring them by his royal Proclamation that they would enjoy along with British subjects the benefits of English law, has promised them that they will have all the advantages of it and that as British subjects they will be allowed to be represented in the House of Assembly by Canadians of their own communion. The Mother Country cannot refuse this favour because it is already allowed to them contrary to its own statutes to be sworn as Jurors not only in civil but also in criminal cases.

The old subjects who are reasonable ... do not oppose such a House of Assembly composed of old and new subjects. ... The inhabitants of this province know that if such a House is established it will be indispensably necessary to impose taxes, to provide for the expenses of government. [But they ask that if taxes are to be imposed the boundary of the province should be extended in order to favour trade.]

It may have been as a result of this paper that committees of English and Canadian merchants did meet in Quebec the following November to prepare a joint petition, but as the English Committee reported, "It is now the general opinion of the people (French and English) that an Assembly would be of the utmost advantage to the Colony, tho' they cannot agree as to the Constitution of it."[33]

NOTES

1 "Articles of capitulation, upon which the country is surrendered, and treaties of peace by which it is ceded, are sacred and inviolate, according to their true intent and meaning." Lord Mansfield's Judgment in Campbell v. Hall, 1774. A. Shortt and A. G. Doughty: *Documents relating to the Constitutional History of Canada 1760-1791* (1918), p. 526 (hereafter cited as S. & D.).

2 English version taken from S. & D., p. 25ff.

3 *Ibid.*, p. 113.

4 *Ibid.*, p. 163.

5 C. W. Alvord, *The Mississippi Valley in British Politics* (Cleveland: Arthur H. Clark Co., 1917), Vol. II; see p. 114. This theory can be found in Advocate General Marriott's report on the laws of Quebec (1773?), S. & D., p. 449. Some scholars believe that the executive clauses of the Proclamation are only those that refer to Indian lands. The clauses quoted below, they suggest, say only what the King has done or will do in virtue of the royal prerogative.

6 S. & D., p. 131.

7 *Ibid.*, p. 168.

8 *Ibid.*, p. 181.

9 *Ibid.*, p. 205.

10 *Ibid.*, p. 212.

11 *Ibid.*, p. 215.

12 *Ibid.*, p. 219.

13 *Ibid.*, p. 231.

14 Murray may have thought of their going to Louisiana. His references are vague.

15 S. & D., p. 227.

16 *Ibid.*, p. 236.

17 *Ibid.*, p. 251.

18 *Canadian Historical Review* XIV (Toronto: University of Toronto Press, 1933). Humphreys, R. A. and Scott, F. M., "Lord Northington and the Laws of Canada," pp. 59-61. The draft instructions are printed as an appendix to the article.

19 Public Archives of Canada (hereafter, PAC), Manuscript Group (M.G.) 23, A1 (8) Dartmouth Papers, 2262.

20 S. & D., p. 522.

21 *Ibid.*, p. 232.

22 *Ibid.*, p. 235.

23 *Ibid.*, pp. 281, 288, 294.

24 Recent work on the operations of the British Parliament in the eighteenth and early nineteenth centuries makes it easier for the student of Canadian history to understand Carleton's doubts and fears about the operations of an Assembly.

25 S. & D., p. 377.

26 Since 1766 Jean-Olivier Briand, known officially as the "Superintendent of the Romish Religion," had been effectively Bishop of the Roman Catholic Church in Quebec. It is difficult to believe that the Board of Trade members were not

32   *The Quebec Act*

aware of this. (For discussion of this point, see editor's comment, pp. 139-40.) They are perhaps implying that Briand's position with its limited powers should be made even more public in order to prevent encroachments in practice. That the proposals of the Board were acceptable then and later is shown by the fact that they were for the most part included in the instructions which accompanied the Quebec Act.

27 S. & D., p. 417.

28 *Ibid.*, p. 421.

29 *Ibid.*, p. 432.

30 *Ibid.*, p. 437.

31 *Ibid.*, p. 445.

32 *PAC Baby Collection (Transcripts), Political Papers,* Vol. XLVIII, 30938. "Address . . . to His Majesty, July 24, 1773." [Editor's translation]

33 S. & D., p. 490.

PART 2

The Preparation and
Passing of the Act

By 1773 the British government was in possession of a considerable number of reports by legal experts beginning with that of April 4, 1776, signed by Yorke and de Grey, and including the reports from Quebec on which the three senior English officials, Wedderburn, Thurlow and Marriott, had made their own reports. That nothing had been done may be partly explained by the instability of British ministries in this period, by their preoccupation with other even more difficult problems such as the administration of the new possessions in India, and also by the fact that any concessions to French and Roman Catholic Quebec such as an enlightened administration might wish to make could easily provoke violent reactions from a less enlightened public.

a. Lord Chancellor Apsley to Lord Dartmouth [July ? 1773].[1]

A note from the Lord Chancellor to the Secretary of State for the colonies does indicate that by this time there was serious concern about the delay in dealing with Quebec.

> Give me leave to intreat your Lordship to keep the settlement of Quebec in Your Mind, and to forward the Completion of it.—It is a disgrace to Government, I had almost said to Humanity, to leave them in their present deplorable Scituation—

On August 4, 1773, Apsley sent Lord Dartmouth the three reports of the British law officers on Quebec saying how happy he was to hear that Dartmouth was going to deal with the Canadian question.[2] A few weeks later Francis Maseres, former Attorney General of Quebec, wrote to Lord Dartmouth stating that Lord North the Prime Minister was determined to carry through an act on Quebec during the next session, and that he did not favour an Assembly but a Council without the power of taxation. Maseres stated also that Lord Mansfield, the Chief Justice, was reading over all papers relating to Quebec and that

Lord Chancellor Apsley was doing the same thing. Maseres therefore suggested to Dartmouth that if he introduced the business to the Privy Council he would get full support from his colleagues.[3]

b. Second [?] Draft of Quebec Bill.[4]

The Dartmouth Papers contain several undated drafts of the Quebec Act. What seems to be the earliest provides for a Council with powers of taxation to continue for fourteen years unless an Assembly should be granted sooner. This was perhaps drafted by Wedderburn.[5] Another draft, perhaps the next, is entitled "An Act to remove the doubts which have arisen relative to the Laws and Government of Quebec . . ." The very long preamble states these doubts in detail and with what may have been considered excessive frankness, as no such statement appears in any other draft. This draft repealed the Proclamation of 1763 insofar as it related to Quebec and also all ordinances passed under its authority, provided for a legislative council and for a basis of civil law in the following words:

> And be it further Enacted by the Authority aforesaid, That His Majesty's Subjects of and in the said Province of Quebec, as the same is described in, and by the said Proclamation and Commissions And also of all the Territories part of the Province of Canada at the time of the Conquest thereof which His Majesty, His Heirs or Successors may think proper to annex to the said Government of Quebec may have hold and enjoy their Property, Laws, Customs, and Usages, in as large, ample and beneficial manner, as if the said Proclamation, Commissions Ordinances and other Acts & Instruments had not been made, and as may consist with their allegiance to His Majesty and subjection to the Crown and Parliament of Great Britain. [Criminal law is to be based on a combination of English and Canadian law.]

c. Third Draft of Quebec Bill: Comment by [Lord Mansfield].[6]

A later draft of the Quebec Bill was apparently worded so as to give rights or privileges to the Roman Catholic Church, and also to give "the Canadians the Enjoyment of their ancient civil Rights, customs and Usages." This draft seems to have included a limiting clause intended to secure special rights to Protestants. All that is known of this bill is derived from an unsigned, undated document endorsed "The Clause Concerning Religion in the Third Draught." The comment has been attributed to Lord Mansfield, and there is evidence to support this attribution. On the other hand one passage suggests that it must have been by Chief Justice Hey.[7]

The Proviso in favour of the Protestant Subjects of Quebec, if it is intended to operate only as a saving to the clause which gives to the Canadians the free exercise of their Religion appears to me to be unnecessary—from a Church merely tolerated, as the Romish Church is by this Act, There can be little occasion to resort to any special protection, immunity or Privilege in behalf of any body, for existing only by Permission of the state, it can claim nothing, enforce nothing, exercise no controul or Authority over its members but by consent, & it should seem useless to reserve to others by express Provision of Law, what cannot be taken from them but by their own choice & approbation.

In this light therefore the clause seems to be unnecessary.

But if it is intended to operate as a saving to the clause immediately preceding which gives the Canadians the Enjoyment of their ancient civil Rights, customs and Usages, I apprehend it will be found an Exception as large as the Rule; and leave it still in doubt, whether in a matter of civil Right the Canadian or English Law where they differ together with the form & mode of Proceeding, shall have the Preference. A Case which came before me in Judgement, & which is very likely to happen again will possibly put the objection I mean to state in a clear light before your Lordship.

[The writer gives an example of a case involving a contract and a mortgage on real property which, if Canadian law were followed, would expose one party to what an Englishman would regard as a severe hardship amounting to a serious injustice. The writer argues that the Englishman could then claim (presumably in the words of the third draft) "Every *Privilege Protection & advantage of what Nature* soever *or kind that* I am intitled to by the Laws & Constitution of the Realm of England, are expressly reserved to me," upon which he would demand a trial by jury, satisfied that a jury would set aside Canadian law and render what he would regard as substantial justice.] . . .

Whatever is to operate as an Exception to a positive general Law ought I apprehend to be clearly & expressly pointed out. it is your

Lordship's Intention (I presume) to revive the whole canadian Law in matters of a civil Nature, to make it the general law of the country to govern british as well as canadian Property by its Rules. if your Lordship intends any reservation with respect either to the Laws or the Administration of them, in favour of the british subjects, it must, I apprehend be clearly ascertained where & in what instances it should take Place. a General reservation like that contained in the clause will either operate nothing, or go to the destruction of the whole. for if the Legislature does not draw the Line I know not well how any Judge can do it.

[The memorandum concludes with the suggestion that "a bare Toleration" for the Roman Catholic religion "without any maintenance or support for the clergy" seems to be intended, and it goes on]:

But will your Lordship (upon reflection) think it sufficient barely to tolerate a large & powerful Body of Men the R.C. Clergy in Canada, in the exercise of their Religion, without any other means of support than what is to arise from the Voluntary contribution of their Parishioners, or does your Lordship apprehend any mischief or great inconvenience would arise from acknowledging their right to a decent & moderate maintenance under the sanction of a british Act of Parliament.

d. The Boundary Clause: Lord Hillsborough's Objections, Dartmouth's Reply.[8]

A later draft of the bill, probably prepared in the spring of 1774, brought it to something very close to its final form. A new preamble was inserted, a clause for the extension of the boundary, a more restricted grant to Canadians of their own civil law and a criminal law exclusively English. Wedderburn in notes on this draft explained that the first preamble and the first enacting clause (on the boundary) were new, that the former preamble "reciting and condemning the Proclamation and other consequential Acts of Government" had been omitted, and that Chief Justice Hey had modified the clauses granting Canadian law because the former wording might have included a body of ecclesiastical law.

Lord Hillsborough, Dartmouth's predecessor as Colonial Secretary, objected to the extension of the boundary and to a clause allowing the granting of land in free and common soccage and allowing anyone over twenty-five years to convert his property from seigneurial to freehold tenure.

The extention of the boundaries to the North so as to comprehend the Labrador coast his Lordship approves, but has insuperable objections to the extention to the Mississippi and Ohio. His reasons as far as I can recollect them are these. If an extention of the boundaries for the sake of Jurisdiction only over the Inhabitants was intended. There is no occasion for doing it by Act of Parliament as it is in the power of the Crown at present to give such jurisdiction if thought fit. And it is better to do it by the authority of the Crown *only*, because the jurisdiction so given may be limited & restrained in such manner as to answer all the purposes of Government and to avoid the inconveniences with which a general extention or annexation will be attended.

But from the Terms in which the extention is made and what is said in the subsequent Clauses his Lordship supposes that it is intended to make Parliament *declare* that it is right and proper to *settle* The Territories annexed, for these Lands & Inhabitants are put in exactly the same state as those within the present Limits. An inducement is held out to the Roman Catholick subjects of Quebec and to all other Roman Catholics to remove into these annexed Countries by granting them the French Laws & Customs of Canada and the Free exercise of their Religion.

His Lordship objects to the granting of any Lands in the Province in free & common Soccage & refers to a Report of the Board of Trade for his reasons for continuing the french mode of Seigneuries as the most fit for the purposes of Government & as corresponding with the whole scope & purpose of the Bill . . .

General Carleton makes the same objections . . . as Lord Hillsborough does, and adds. . . . That the Tenure by Seigneurie gives the Crown great power over the Seigneur, which power will be done away by changing the Tenure into free & common Soccage. That the Evil disposed Seigneurs will therefore be the first to avail themselves of the permission to change their Tenures in order to get rid of that power and be able to do mischief with less restraint.

On May 1, 1774, Dartmouth wrote to Hillsborough[9] as follows:

My Dear Lord . . . the Cabinet . . . are unanimously of opinion that the extension of the Province to the Ohio & Mississippi, is an essential & very useful part of the Bill; it provides for the establishment of civil government over many numerous settlements of french subjects, but does by no means imply an intention of further settling the Lands included within this extension, & if it is not wished that British Subjects should settle that country nothing can more effectually tend to discourage such attempts, wch in the present state of that Country, y^r Lord^p knows very well, it is impossible to prevent. Y^r objection to The clause allowing a change of Tenure their Lord^ps thought proper to come into & it is accordingly struck out of the Bill.

e. The Quebec Bill: Debates in the House of Commons, May 26-June 13, 1774.[10]

During the debates on the Quebec Bill, Carleton, Hey, Maseres and others gave evidence. The most contentious issues were the use of Canadian civil law and the refusal of an assembly, although there were criticisms of the boundary extension and questions as to how far the religious provisions "established" the Roman Catholic Church.

Lord North—The honourable gentleman next demands of us, will you extend into those countries the free exercise of the Romish religion? Upon my word, Sir, I do not see that this bill extends it further than the ancient limits of Canada; but if it should do so, the country to which it is extended is the habitation of bears and beavers. . . . The general purpose is undoubtedly to give a legislature to that country . . . but can a better legislature be given than that of a governor and council? . . . The bulk of the inhabitants are Roman Catholics, and to subject them to an assembly composed of a few British subjects would be a great hardship. Being, therefore, under the necessity of not appointing an assembly, this is the only legislature you can give the Canadians, and it is the one under which they live at present . . .

Now, Sir, with regard to giving French law—if gentlemen will remember, the most material part of the criminal law is to be according to English law. . . . It has been thought better calculated to secure the happiness of Canadians, and more beneficial for all who live in the country, that they should have the civil law of Canada, and not that of England. If the Canadian civil law is incompatible with the present condition and wishes of the colony, the governor and council will have power to alter it. But there must be a general basis; there must be a law established, ready to be amended and altered as occasions shall arise, and as the circumstances of the colony shall require. It has been the opinion of very many able lawyers, that the best way to establish the happiness of the inhabitants is to give them their own laws, as far as relates to their own possessions. . . . the criminal law has been submitted to for nine years, and is, I dare say, approved of by the Canadians, because it is a more refined and a more merciful law than the law of France.[11]

Colonel Barré in his speech hinted at a motive which was a matter of debate from the passing of the Bill until the present century.

I look upon this measure as bad in itself, and as leading to something worse; that I foresee it will not contribute to the peace of the country for which it is intended; and that it carries in its breast something that squints and looks dangerous to the inhabitants of our other colonies in that country.

Solicitor General Wedderburn suggested an interesting change of attitude in Great Britain from the time of the Proclamation of 1763. It had then been expected that many from the American colonies would settle in Canada. It was now known that they were not likely to do so. Wedderburn had the attitude of the mercantilist that British traders might reside abroad temporarily, but that the expanding industries of the country made it desirable to keep the population at home. It will be remembered that only about the middle of the eighteenth century did the natural increase of the population begin to compete successfully with its two great enemies, famine and disease.

I have hitherto, Sir, in all that I have said, considered the Canadian inhabitants as the object of the legislature. A great deal has been said with regard to the British subjects settled in Canada. Now, I confess, that the situation of the British settler is not the principal object of my attention. I do not wish to see Canada draw from this country any considerable number of her inhabitants. I think there ought to be no temptation held out to the subjects of England to quit their native soil, to increase colonies at the expence of this country. If persons have gone thither in the course of trade, they have gone without any intention of making it their permanent residence; and, in that case, it is no more a hardship to tell them, "this is the law of the land," than it would be to say so to a man whose affairs induced him to establish himself in Guernsey, or in any other part of North America. . . . With regard to the other portion of the inhabitants of North America, I think the consideration alters; if the geographical limits are rightly stated, I think one great advantage of the extension of territory is this, that they will have little temptation to stretch themselves northward. I would not say, "cross the Ohio, you will find the Utopia of some great and mighty empire." I would say, "this is the border, beyond which, for the advantage of the whole empire, you shall not extend yourselves." . . .

Edmund Burke, like Colonel Barré, implied a connection between the Quebec Act and Britain's current dispute with the American colonies.

. . . I stand for the necessity of information; without which—without great, cogent, luminous information—I, for one, will never give my vote for establishing the French law in that country. I should be sorry to see his Majesty a despotic governor. And am I sure that this despotism is not meant to lead to universal despotism? When that country cannot be governed as a free country, I question whether this can. No free country can keep another country in slavery. The price they pay for it will be their own servitude. The constitution proposed is one which men never will, and never ought to bear. When we are sowing the seeds of despotism in Canada, let us bear in mind, that it is a growth which may afterwards extend to other countries. By being made perpetual, it is evident that this constitution is meant to be both an instrument of tyranny in the Canadians, and an example to others of what they have to expect. At some time or other it will come home to England.

Francis Maseres in his evidence, although he himself was opposed to an assembly, acknowledged that some at least of the Canadians would have liked to have one.

. . . What do you understand to be the sentiments of the Canadians with regard to the form of government they would wish to live under?—I have not heard many of the Canadians enter fully into the subject. I believe their opinion is that of our poet, "Whate'er is best administer'd is best." They have no predilection at present in favour of a legislative council, or in favour of an assembly: I speak of the generality of the people. There are a few persons who have thought more upon the subject than the rest: I believe they would incline to an assembly.

William Hey, who had been Chief Justice of Quebec since 1766, explained his preference for a somewhat more modest introduction of Canadian civil law than the one provided by the Quebec Act.

... Do you think it would be impracticable, or even very difficult to draw such a line of admission of Canadian laws, as would give satisfaction both to the new and old subjects?—I myself have been unfortunate enough to differ with General Carleton in that respect. His Majesty was pleased to order the governor, the attorney-general, and myself, to make our report upon the state of the province, and particularly with regard to grievances which the Canadians either felt, or thought they felt, under the administration of justice, as it was then administered; together with the remedies that we thought most proper to be applied to those grievances. The Canadians conceived that the introduction of the English laws, and the exclusion of their own, at least their doubt and uncertainty how far that matter went, was their greatest grievance; and the remedy proposed to be applied was the restoration of their own laws and customs *in toto.* I own, myself, I thought that went too far. I thought that such a mixture might be made, as would be agreeable both to the Canadians and British subjects, at least the reasonable part of both, and answer every purpose of state policy here at home. ... I was willing to allow [the Canadians] the whole law with respect to their tenures, with respect to the alienation, descent, and mode of conveying or incumbering their real property, to the rights of dower and marriage, and the disposition of their personal estate in case of intestacy. This I thought was a very large field for them: quieting and securing their possessions according to their own notions of property, and not breaking in upon or disturbing their former settlements. The rest of the law, as the law respecting contracts, debts, disputes of a commercial nature, the law of evidence, and, any other matters of that kind, I thought I might safely stand upon English bottom. These, with the whole criminal law of England, with the trial by jury, the presentment by the grand inquest, together with the establishment or at least, toleration of their religion, with some reformation in the proceedings of the courts of justice ... would, I had hoped, have made up a system that should not reasonably have been objected to by either British or Canadians. I am of opinion, that at the time I stated that as the ground of my difference from General Carleton's report it would have been satisfactory to the Canadians. I am in doubt now whether it will; but I still think it ought.

Why do you think it would not now be satisfactory to the Canadians?—I apprehend they have risen in their demands of late, and hope to be gratified to the utmost extent of their desires.

Upon what are these very extensive opinions founded? I know of no particular ground for the extent of them. It appears to be a natural progressive state from the condition they were in, to that in which they now stand. They were terrified, and in a state almost of distraction. They neither expected to retain their religion or their laws, and looked upon themselves as a ruined and abandoned people; but when they saw attention wisely and humanely paid to their situation, they were willing to improve their condition, as far as their ideas carried them, to the absolute restitution of their whole laws and customs. But I know of no particular encouragement given them to ask anything. It was, I have no doubt, promised them, that their case should be fully and fairly represented, and that they might rely upon his Majesty's bounty and goodness for their relief . . .

Do you conceive the Canadians would have any great objection to a provincial assembly, into which Roman Catholics would be admitted, under certain restrictions, such as taking the oaths?—I believe they have no idea of advantage from it. They look upon the house of assembly as a house of riot, calculated for nothing but to disturb the government, and obstruct public servants.

Do they understand that there is a resemblance between the house of assembly and the House of Commons in this country?—They do not understand the principles of either.

Charles James Fox, like Burke and Barré, as an opponent of the government's American policy pleaded for an Assembly.

. . . My objection to the bill consists mainly in my objection to this clause: it begins by stating, that "it is at present inexpedient to call an assembly." . . . I am free to say, that the Canadians are my first object; and I maintain, that their happiness and their liberties are the proper objects, and ought to be the leading principle, of this bill; but how these are to be secured to them without an assembly, I cannot see. It is not in nature for men to love laws, by which their rights and liberties are not protected. I must have more substantial evidence before I consent to establish arbitrary power in that country: before I consent to establish such a government upon the principle, that *volenti non fit injuria*, I must be exceedingly well assured of the *volens*. . . . No one has urged the circumstance of the people of Canada being Roman Catholics as an objection to an assembly; and I trust I shall never hear such an objection stated; for no one who has ever conversed with Roman Catholics can, I think, believe that there is anything repugnant, in their views, to the principles of political freedom. The principles of political freedom, though not practised in Roman Catholic countries, are as much cherished and revered by the people, as in Protestant countries. If there was danger, I should look for it more from those of high rank, than those of low.

f. Comment of a Canadian Seigneur on the Quebec Act.[12]

The seigneur Chartier de Lotbinière, who had given evidence during the debates on the Bill, was not satisfied with it in its final form, believing that it deprived Canadians of some law that they valued and left in danger even what was conceded to them.

> . . . shall the governor have the right to make statutes which might annul the fundamental laws of Canada? . . . Should his process not rather be restricted to only making police regulations, and that strictly in accordance with the fundamental laws of the country without ever being able to step outside the spirit of these laws, such as the governor general and the Intendant of police were able to make in the aforesaid country for regulations of minor importance, and these two were in combination with the superior council for matters of greater importance . . . What I can state as positively certain is that in the request [the Canadians] are making for their own laws, there is no question of excepting such of them as relate, to criminals; and they would not have failed to express their opinion if they had preferred the English law on this point. . . . Besides the Canadian understands the criminal law which has been followed from the beginning in this country; he will not perhaps fully understand the law which it is sought to substitute for it, and is there a more painful situation for the thoughtful man, than never to know whether he is worthy of praise or blame. He believes too that he can see a danger, under the English law, of his being looked upon as a criminal, on the bare oath of a man, without any offence or crime being proved . . . This is the most fearful danger that it is possible to imagine, and one to which the Canadian is certain never to be exposed under the

French law. As to the evidence during trial, and the proofs required to establish his guilt, and to subject him to the penalty for it, he knows that by the mode of procedure according to the French laws, the minutest precautions are most scrupulously observed, and that he can only be condemned on proofs as clear as the day. There remains then nothing else to cite to the advantage of the English criminal, except the satisfaction of being condemned by twelve jurors, who are called his peers. Is it credible that the Canadian, or anyone else who wished to divest himself of the prejudices of his childhood, would believe that he would be exposed to more favouritism, to more injustice, and to less enlightenment, if he were judged by a Court composed of twelve judges chosen from the class of the most honourable men in the province all thoroughly acquainted with the law (such as formed the superior council of this country under the French government, and which it is absolutely imperative to re-establish, if it is desired to insure the life, the property, and the fortune of the citizens) . . .

With regard to the establishment of the legislative power in Canada, I have already had occasion to demonstrate to the honourable chamber how essential it was to entrust it only to the largest landed proprietors in this country; owners only of properties recognized all over the world as solid, any others being liable to ruin from a sudden fire, or a few bankruptcies. It is from them only we can hope for the attention and care necessary to foresee the evil, and to develop all the natural advantages which the country may possess, seeing that they are the most prominent and the most interested in the success of the matter: this cannot reasonably be expected from those who have no interest, or only a very slight one in the public good, and especially if their personal interests are opposed to public ones.

A brief comment by Chief Justice Hey on this matter in a letter to the Lord Chancellor written January 25, 1774, is of interest.[13]

. . . And I much doubt whether the Canadians themselves are not, upon the whole, better satisfied with our modes of administring the criminal Law, & even with the Law itself as far as they know it, than their own. The pride of a few haughty seigneurs may perhaps revolt at the Idea of submitting their conduct to the decision of a Rank of men they are too apt upon all occasions to despise, but their high Ideas of Honour and Justice, it is to be presumed will for ever exempt them from being the subject of such an Institution as the Trial by Jury, and their speculative opinions upon it are in my mind worthey of very little consideration or Indulgence.

Hey, however, made a concession to the attitude of Chartier de Lotbinière in the same letter in which he expressed to the Lord Chancellor his anxiety about the quality of the men on the bench. He pointed out that those who had served in that capacity in Quebec had no professional training or previous experience and that it was of the utmost importance to send out "two Gentlemen of ability & Character with a proper Appointment, (I should prefer civilians[14] to common Lawyers)."

NOTES

[1] PAC, Dartmouth Papers (Patshull), Series 3, Vol. 2, p. 1.

[2] S. & D., p. 534, fn.

[3] *Ibid.*, p. 534, fn.

[4] *Ibid.*, p. 536.

[5] *Ibid.*, p. 535, fn. 1.

[6] *Ibid.*, p. 549. Readers who refer to Shortt and Doughty should notice the inconsistency in their description of the drafts. The comments here cannot possibly refer to the so-called "Third Draft" (p. 543).

[7] The original in the Dartmouth Papers is attributed to Hey (by an unknown writer). It is almost certainly in Hey's handwriting.

[8] S. & D., p. 551 and fn. 2.

[9] *Ibid.*, p. 554.

[10] W. P. M. Kennedy, *Statutes, Treaties and Documents of the Canadian Constitution 1713-1929* (Toronto: Oxford University Press, 1930), p. 94ff.

[11] This in present day jargon was a "value judgment." More precisely, Lord North is expressing his own preference, assuming that it will be shared by Canadians, forgetting that, whatever the relative merits of rival systems may be, people generally prefer the ills they know. The English objections to French procedure were based on their dislike of the inquisitorial system, a dislike which Canadians could hardly be expected to share; and objection to the use of torture to obtain a confession (or to confirm one); and to the brutality of French modes of execution. It would be hard to imagine a more revolting form of execution than the English hanging, drawing and quartering, although the pains of death on the French wheel would be much more prolonged. Here the preference would depend largely on the way in which the law was customarily applied. In England, and apparently in France, the executioner might deliberately shorten the death agonies. This executive mercy

could not be counted on, but was apparently generally practised in New France. The fact remains, however, that there is no evidence that Canadians challenged statements like this one of Lord North, or that any but Chartier du Lotbinière seriously disapproved the introduction of English criminal law (see p. 43).

12 S. & D., p. 564.

13 Chief Justice Hey to the Lord Chancellor, Jan. 25, 1774. PAC, Dartmouth Papers (Patshull), II, No. 941.

14 French and Canadian law were based on Roman "civil" as opposed to English "common" law; hence Hey asks for "civilians" rather than "common" lawyers.

PART 3

The Quebec Act[1]

ANNO DECIMO QUARTO
GEORGII III. REGIS
CAP. LXXXIII.

An Act for making more effectual Provision for the Government of the Province of *Quebec* in *North America*.

Whereas His Majesty, by His Royal Proclamation, Preamble. bearing Date the Seventh Day of *October*, in the Third Year of His Reign, thought fit to declare the Provisions which had been made in respect to certain Countries, Territories, and Islands in *America*, ceded to His Majesty by the definitive Treaty of Peace, concluded at *Paris* on the Tenth Day of *February*, One thousand seven hundred and sixty-three: And whereas, by the Arrangements made by the said Royal Proclamation, a very large Extent of Country, within which there were several Colonies and Settlements of the Subjects of *France*, who claimed to remain therein under the Faith of the said Treaty, was left, without any Provision being made for the Administration of Civil Government therein; and certain Parts of the Territory of *Canada*, where sedentary Fisheries had been established and carried on by the Subjects of *France*, Inhabitants of the said Province of *Canada*, under Grants and Concessions from the Government thereof, were annexed to the Government of *Newfoundland*, and thereby subjected to Regulations inconsistent with the Nature of such Fisheries: May it therefore please Your most Excellent Majesty that it may be enacted; and be it enacted by the King's most Excellent Majesty, by and with the Advice and Consent of the Lords Spiritual and Temporal, and Commons, in this present Parliament assembled, and by the Authority of the same, That all the Territories, Islands, and Countries in *North America*, belonging to the Crown of *Great Britain*, bounded on the South by a Line from the Bay of *Chaleurs*, along the High Lands which divide the Rivers that empty themselves into the River *Saint Lawrence* from those which fall into the Sea, to a Point in Forty-five Degrees of Northern Latitude, on the Eastern Bank of the River *Connecticut*, keeping the same Latitude directly West, through the Lake *Champlain*, until, in the same Latitude, it meets the River *Saint Lawrence*; from thence up the Eastern Bank of the said River to the Lake *Ontario*; thence through the Lake *Ontario*, and the River commonly called *Niagara*; and thence along by the Eastern and South-eastern Bank of Lake *Erie*, following the said Bank, until the same shall be intersected by the Northern Boundary, granted by the Charter of the Province of *Pennsylvania*, in case the same shall be so intersected; and from thence along the said Northern and Western Boundaries of the said Province, until the said Western Boundary strike the *Ohio*: But in case the said Bank of the said Lake shall not be found to be so intersected, then following the said Bank until it shall arrive at that Point of the said Bank which shall be nearest to the North-western Angle of the said Province of *Pennsylvania*, and thence, by a right Line, to the said North-western Angle of the said Province; and thence along the Western Boundary of the said Province, until it strike the River *Ohio*; and along the Bank of the said River, Westward, to the Banks of the *Mississippi*, and Northward to the Southern Boundary of the Territory granted to the Merchants Adventurers of *England*, trading to *Hudson's Bay*; and also all such Territories, Islands, and Countries, which have, since the Tenth of *February*, One thousand seven hundred and sixty-three, been made Part of the Government of *Newfoundland*, be, and they are hereby, during His Majesty's Pleasure, annexed to, and made Part and Parcel of, the Province of *Quebec*, as created and established by the said Royal Proclamation of the Seventh of *October*, One thousand seven hundred and sixty-three.

The Territories, Islands, and Countries, in North America, *belonging to* Great Britain.

annexed to the Province of Quebec.

Provided always, That nothing herein contained, relative to the Boundary of the Province of *Quebec*, shall in anywise affect the Boundaries of any other Colony.

Provided always, and be it enacted, That nothing in this Act contained shall extend, or be construed to extend, to make void, or to vary or alter any Right, Title, or Possession, derived under any Grant, Conveyance, or otherwise howsoever, of or to any Lands within the said Province, or the Provinces thereto adjoining; but that the same shall remain and be in Force, and have Effect, as if this Act had never been made.

And whereas the Provisions, made by the said Proclamation, in respect to the Civil Government of the said Province of *Quebec*, and the Powers and Authorities given to the Governor and other Civil Officers of the said Province, by the Grants and Commissions issued in consequence thereof, have been found, upon Experience, to be inapplicable to the State and Circumstances of the said Province, the Inhabitants whereof amounted, at the Conquest, to above Sixty-five thousand Persons professing the Religion of the Church of *Rome*, and enjoying an established Form of Constitution and System of Laws, by which their Persons and Property had been protected, governed, and ordered, for a long Series of Years, from the First Etablishment of the said Province of *Canada*; be it therefore further enacted by the Authority aforesaid, That the said Proclamation, so far as the same relates to the said Province of *Quebec,* and the Commission under the Authority whereof the Government of the said Province is at present administered, and all and every the Ordinance and Ordinances made by the Governor and Council of *Quebec* for the Time being, relative to the Civil Government and Administration of Justice in the said Province, and all Commissions to Judges and other Officers thereof, be, and the same are hereby revoked, annulled, and made void, from and after the First Day of *May*, One thousand seven hundred and seventy-five.

And, for the more perfect Security and Ease of the Minds of the Inhabitants of the said Province, it is hereby declared, That His Majesty's Subjects, professing the

Not to affect the Boundaries of any other Colony;

nor to make void other Rights formerly granted

Former Provisions made for the Province to be null and void after *May 1, 1775.*

Inhabitants of *Quebec* may profess

the Romish Religion, subject to the King's Supremacy, as by Act I Eliz; and the Clergy enjoy their accustomed Dues.

Religion of the Church of *Rome* of and in the said Province of *Quebec*, may have, hold, and enjoy, the free Exercise of the Religion of the Church of *Rome*, subject to the King's Supremacy, declared and established by an Act, made in the First Year of the Reign of Queen *Elizabeth*, over all the Dominions and Countries which then did, or thereafter should belong, to the Imperial Crown of this Realm; and that the Clergy of the said Church may hold, receive, and enjoy, their accustomed Dues and Rights, with respect to such Persons only as shall profess the said Religion.

Provision may be made by His Majesty for the Support of the Protestant Clergy.

Provided nevertheless, That it shall be lawful for His Majesty, His Heirs or Successors, to make such Provision out of the rest of the said accustomed Dues and Rights, for the Encouragement of the Protestant Religion, and for the Maintenance and Support of a Protestant Clergy within the said Province, as he or they shall, from Time to Time, think necessary and expedient.

No person professing the Romish Religion obliged to take the Oath of I Eliz.; but to take, before the Governor, &c., the following Oath.

Provided always, and be it enacted, That no Person, professing the Religion of the Church of *Rome*, and residing in the said Province, shall be obliged to take the Oath required by the said Statute passed in the First Year of the Reign of Queen *Elizabeth*, or any other Oaths substituted by any other Act in the Place thereof; but that every such Person who, by the said Statute is required to take the Oath therein mentioned, shall be obliged, and is hereby required, to take and subscribe the following Oath before the Governor, or such other Person in such Court of Record as His Majesty shall appoint, who are hereby authorized to administer the same; *videlicet,*

The Oath.

I A. B. *do sincerely promise and swear, That I will be faithful, and bear true Allegiance to His Majesty King* GEORGE, *and him will defend to the utmost of my Power, against all traiterous Conspiracies, and Attempts whatsoever, which shall be made against His Person, Crown, and Dignity; and I will do my utmost Endeavour to disclose and make known to His Majesty, His Heirs and Successors, all Treasons, and traiterous Conspiracies,*

*and Attempts, which I shall know to be against Him, or
any of Them; and all this I do swear without any Equi-
vocation, mental Evasion, or secret Reservation, and re-
nouncing all Pardons and Dispensations from any Power
or Person whomsoever to the Contrary.*

SO HELP ME GOD.

And every such Person, who shall neglect or refuse to
take the said Oath before mentioned, shall incur and be
liable to the same Penalties, Forfeitures, Disabilities, and
Incapacities, as he would have incurred and been liable
to for neglecting or refusing to take the Oath required by
the said Statute passed in the First Year of the Reign of
Queen *Elizabeth.*

And be it further enacted by the Authority aforesaid,
That all His Majesty's *Canadian* Subjects, within the
Province of *Quebec*, the religious Orders and Communities only excepted, may also hold and enjoy their Property and Possessions, together with all Customs and
Usages relative thereto, and all other their Civil Rights,
in as large, ample, and beneficial Manner, as if the said
Proclamation, Commissions, Ordinances, and other Acts
and Instruments, had not been made, and as may consist
with their Allegiance to His Majesty, and Subjection to
the Crown and Parliament of *Great Britain*; and that in
all Matters of Controversy, relative to Property and Civil
Rights, Resort shall be had to the Laws of *Canada,* as the
Rule for the Decision of the same; and all Causes that
shall hereafter be instituted in any of the Courts of Justice, to be appointed within and for the said Province, by
His Majesty, His Heirs and Successors, shall, with respect to such Property and Rights, be determined agree-
ably to the said Laws and Customs of *Canada*, until they
shall be varied or altered by any Ordinances that shall,
from Time to Time, be passed in the said Province by the
Governor, Lieutenant Governor, or Commander in
Chief, for the Time being, by and with the Advice and
Consent of the Legislative Council of the same, to be
appointed in Manner herein-after mentioned.

Persons re-
fusing the
Oath to be
subject to the
Penalties by
Act I *Eliz.*

His Majesty's
Canadian
Subjects
(religious
Orders ex-
cepted) may
hold all their
Possessions,
etc.

and in
Matters of
Controversy,
Resort to be
had to the
Laws of
Canada for
the Decision.

Not to extend to Lands granted by His Majesty in common Soccage.

Provided always, That nothing in this Act contained shall extend, or be construed to extend, to any Lands that have been granted by His Majesty, or shall hereafter be granted by His Majesty, His Heirs and Successors, to be holden in free and common Soccage.

Owners of Goods may alienate the same by Will, &c.

if executed according to the Laws of *Canada.*

Provided also, That it shall and may be lawful to and for every Person that is Owner of any Lands, Goods, or Credits, in the said Province, and that has a Right to alienate the said Lands, Goods, or Credits, in his or her Life-time, by Deed of Sale, Gift, or otherwise, to devise or bequeath the same at his or her Death, by his or her last Will and Testament; any Law, Usage, or Custom, heretofore or now prevailing in the Province, to the Contrary hereof in any-wise notwithstanding; such Will being executed, either according to the Laws of Canada, or according to the Forms prescribed by the Laws of *England.*

Criminal Law of *England* to be continued in the Province.

And whereas the Certainty and Lenity of the Criminal Law of *England*, and the Benefits and Advantages resulting from the Use of it, have been sensibly felt by the Inhabitants, from an Experience of more than Nine Years, during which it has been uniformly administered; be it therefore further enacted by the Authority aforesaid, That the same shall continue to be administered, and shall be observed as Law in the Province of *Quebec*, as well in the Description and Quality of the Offence as in the Method of Prosecution and Trial; and the Punishments and Forfeitures thereby inflicted to the Exclusion of every other Rule of Criminal Law, or Mode of Proceeding thereon, which did or might prevail in the said Province before the Year of our Lord One thousand seven hundred and sixty-four; any Thing in this Act to the Contrary thereof in any Respect notwithstanding; subject nevertheless to such Alterations and Amendments as the Governor, Lieutenant-governor, or Commander in Chief for the Time being, by and with the Advice and Consent of the legislative Council of the said Province, hereafter to be appointed, shall, from Time to Time, cause to be made therein, in Manner herein-after directed.

And whereas it may be necessary to ordain many Regulations for the future Welfare and good Government of the Province of *Quebec*, the Occasions of which cannot now be foreseen, nor, without much Delay and Inconvenience, be provided for, without intrusting that Authority, for a certain Time, and under proper Restrictions, to Persons resident there: And whereas it is at present inexpedient to call an Assembly; be it therefore enacted by the Authority aforesaid, That it shall and may be lawful for His Majesty, His Heirs and Successors, by Warrant under His or Their Signet or Sign Manual, and with the Advice of the Privy Council, to constitute and appoint a Council for the Affairs of the Province of *Quebec,* to consist of such Persons resident there, not exceeding Twenty-three, nor less than Seventeen, as His Majesty, His Heirs and Successors, shall be pleased to appoint; and, upon the Death, Removal, or Absence of any of the Members of the said Council, in like Manner to constitute and appoint such and so many other Person or Persons as shall be necessary to supply the Vacancy or Vacancies; which Council, so appointed and nominated, or the major Part thereof, shall have Power and Authority to make Ordinances for the Peace, Welfare, and good Government, of the said Province, with the Consent of His Majesty's Governor, or, in his Absence, of the Lieutenant-governor, or Commander in Chief for the Time being.

Provided always, That nothing in this Act contained shall extend to authorise or impower the said legislative Council to lay any Taxes or Duties within the said Province, such Rates and Taxes only excepted as the Inhabitants of any Town or District within the said Province may be authorised by the said Council to assess, levy, and apply, within the said Town or District, for the Purpose of making Roads, erecting and repairing publick Buildings, or for any other Purpose respecting the local Convenience and Oeconomy of such Town or District.

Provided also, and be it enacted by the Authority aforesaid, That every Ordinance so to be made, shall, within Six Months, be transmitted by the Governor, or,

His Majesty may appoint a Council for the Affairs of the Province;

which Council may make Ordinances, with Consent of the Governor.

The Council are not impowered to lay Taxes, Publick Roads or Buildings excepted. Ordinances made to be laid before His Majesty for His Approbation.

in his Absence, by the Lieutenant-governor, or Commander in Chief for the Time being, and laid before His Majesty for His Royal Approbation; and if His Majesty shall think fit to disallow thereof, the same shall cease and be void from the Time that His Majesty's Order in Council thereupon shall be promulgated at *Quebec.*

Ordinances touching Religion not to be in Force without His Majesty's Approbation.

Provided also, That no Ordinance touching Religion, or by which any Punishment may be inflicted greater than Fine or Imprisonment for Three Months, shall be of any Force or Effect, until the same shall have received His Majesty's Approbation.

When Ordinances are to be passed by a Majority.

Provided also, That no Ordinance shall be passed at any Meeting of the Council where less than a Majority of the whole Council is present, or at any Time except between the First Day of *January* and the First Day of *May*, unless upon some urgent Occasion, in which Case every Member thereof resident at *Quebec*, or within Fifty Miles thereof, shall be personally summoned by the Governor, or, in his Absence, by the Lieutenant-governor, or Commander in Chief for the Time being, to attend the same.

Nothing to hinder His Majesty to constitute Courts of Criminal, Civil, and Ecclesiastical Jurisdiction.

And be it further enacted by the Authority aforesaid, That nothing herein contained shall extend, or be construed to extend, to prevent or hinder His Majesty, His Heirs and Successors, by His or Their Letters Patent under the Great Seal of *Great Britain*, from erecting, constituting, and appointing, such Courts of Criminal, Civil, and Ecclesiastical Jurisdiction within and for the said Province of *Quebec*, and appointing, from Time to Time, the Judges and Officers thereof, as His Majesty, His Heirs and Successors, shall think necessary and proper for the Circumstances of the said Province.

All Acts formerly made are hereby inforced within the Province.

Provided always, and it is hereby enacted, That nothing in this Act contained shall extend, or be construed to extend, to repeal or make void, within the said Province of *Quebec*, any Act or Acts of the Parliament of *Great Britain* heretofore made, for prohibiting, restraining, or regulating, the Trade or Commerce of His Majesty's Colonies and Plantations in *America*; but that all and every the said Acts, and also all Acts of Parlia-

ment heretofore made concerning or respecting the said
Colonies and Plantations, shall be, and are hereby declared to be, in Force, within the said Province of *Quebec*, and every Part thereof.

Finis.

NOTES

[1] S. & D., p. 570. A footnote on this page runs as follows: "The text of the Act
is taken from the original folio black letter form in which it was first issued
by the King's Printers. 'London: Printed by Charles Eyre and William
Strachan, Printers to the King's Most Excellent Majesty. MDCCLXXIV.'"

PART 4

Contemporary Interpretation
of the Act

One of the difficulties in arriving at an understanding of the policy and intention of the Quebec Act and of its appropriateness to the colony was that the time of its passage coincided with an acute crisis in the relations between Britain and the other American colonies, and its coming into force coincided in time almost exactly with the opening of hostilities in the American Revolutionary War. It seems quite certain that the Act would have been applied in a different way but for the prolonged constitutional crisis and war in North America in the years after 1774.

a. Appeal of the Continental Congress.[1]

The Quebec Act was associated in the minds of many in the colonies with the acts passed about the same time in Britain in response to the Boston Tea Riot of December 1773. The Continental Congress as a result entered on its journals an appeal from the British Parliament to the British people, reminding them of these repressive acts and of their apparent culmination in the Quebec Act.

Now mark the progression of the ministerial plan for inslaving us.

Well aware that such hardy attempts to take our property from us; to deprive us of that valuable right of trial by jury; to seize our persons, and carry us for trial to Great-Britain; to blockade our ports; to destroy our Charters, and change our forms of government, would occasion, and had already occasioned, great discontent in all the Colonies, which might produce opposition to these measures: An Act was passed to protect, indemnify, and screen from punishment such as might be guilty even of murder, in endeavouring to carry their oppressive edicts into execution; And by another Act the dominion of Canada is to be so extended, modelled, and governed, as that by being disunited from us, detached from our interests, by civil as well as religious prejudices, that by their numbers daily swelling with Catholic emigrants from Europe, and by their devotion to Administration, so friendly to their religion, they might become formidable to us, and on occasion, be fit instruments in the hands of power, to reduce the ancient free Protestant Colonies to the same state of slavery with themselves.

This was evidently the object of the Act:—And in this view, being extremely dangerous to our liberty and quiet, we cannot forebear complaining of it, as hostile to British America.—Superadded to these considerations, we cannot help deploring the unhappy condition to which it has reduced the many English settlers, who, encouraged by the Royal Proclamation, promising the enjoyment of all their rights, have purchased estates in that country.—They are now the subjects of an arbitrary government, deprived of trial by jury, and when imprisoned cannot claim the benefit of the habeas corpus Act, that great bulwark and palladium of English liberty:— Nor can we suppress our astonishment, that a British Parliament should ever consent to establish in that country a religion that has deluged your island in blood, and dispersed impiety, bigotry, persecution, murder and rebellion through every part of the world.

b. Further Response of the Canadians to the Quebec Act.

Carleton's optimism about the Canadian response to the Quebec Act was premature. During the winter when the threat of war with the colonies forced him to consider whether he could, as he had hoped, enlist the Canadians for the defense of the province, he found that the expressions of gratitude which he had received from "all ranks" were no guarantee of subsequent acts of devotion.

The Canadians in General have been made very happy by the Act passed in their Favor, all that have spoke, or wrote to me upon the subject, express the most grateful Sense of what has been done for them; I must not however conceal from Your Excellency, that the Gentry, well disposed, and heartily desirous as they are, to serve the Crown, and to serve it with Zeal, when formed into regular Corps, do not relish commanding a bare Militia, they were never used to

that Service under the French Government . . . As to the Habitants
or Peasantry, ever since the Civil Authority has been introduced
into the Province, the Government of it has hung so loose, and retained so little Power, they have in a Manner emancipated themselves, and it will require Time and discreet Management likewise,
to recall them to their ancient habits of Obedience and Discipline;
. . . (Carleton to Gage, Feb. 4, 1775)[2]

A few months later Chief Justice Hey, writing home to the Lord
Chancellor Apsley, was even more frank.

. . . what will be Your Lordship's astonishment when I tell you
that an act passed for the express purpose of gratifying the Canadians & which was supposed to comprehend all that they either
wished or wanted is become the first object of their discontent &
dislike. English officers to command them in time of war, & English
Laws to govern them in time of Peace, is the general wish. the former they know to be impossible (at least at present) & by the latter if
I understand them right, they mean no Laws & no Government
whatsoever—in the mean time it may be truly said that Gen. Carleton had taken an ill measure of the influence of the seigneurs &
Clergy over the lower order of people whose Principle of conduct
founded in fear & the sharpness of authority over them now no
longer exercised, is unrestrained, & breaks out in every shape of
contempt or detestation of those whom they used to behold with
terror & who gave them I believe too many occasions to express it.
And they on their parts have been and are too much elated with the
advantages they supposed they should derive from the restoration of
their old Priviledges & customs, & indulged themselves in a way of
thinking & talking that gave very just offence, as well to their own
People as to the English merchants . . . (Hey to the Lord Chancellor, Aug. 28, 1775)[3]

c. Dartmouth's Interpretation of the Quebec Act.

Meanwhile, the Earl of Dartmouth, assuming Canadian satisfaction,
was concerned with the opinions of the English minority. The Act was
to come into force on May 1, 1775. Carleton having returned to re-
sume his duties in Quebec, the government then framed the instructions which would be sent to him in the course of the winter. These

instructions would require him to make considerable concessions to what were believed to be the wishes and needs of the merchant group. A plan for the administration of justice was also being drawn up which the Legislative Council would be asked to pass as soon as it was constituted under the Quebec Act. Dartmouth's letter of December 10, 1774, in answer to one of Carleton's of the previous September implies that Carleton knew of these instructions and had been expected to reassure the English by conveying to them at least something of their nature.

As you are silent as to the Sentiments of His Majesty's Natural born Subjects in Canada respecting the late Act, I am not at liberty to conclude that they entertain the same opinion of it, but the King trusts that when the Provisions of it have taken place and His Majesty's gracious Intentions with respect to the Plan of Judicature that is to be established are well known, prejudices which popular Clamour has excited, will cease, and that His Majesty's Subjects of every description will see and be convinced of the Equity and good Policy of the Bill.

It will be your Care, Sir, at the same time you express to the King's new adopted Subjects His Majesty's gracious approbation of the Affection and Respect they have shewn for His Government, to endeavour by every Argument which your own good sense will suggest to you, to persuade the natural born subjects of the justice & propriety of the present form of Government and of the attention that has been shewn to their Interests not only in the adoption of the English Laws, as far as it was consistent with what was due to the just Claims and moderate. Wishes of the Canadians, but in the opening to the British Merchant, by an Extension of the Province, so many new Channels of important Commerce.[4]

The instructions in their final form were dated January 3, 1775. Particularly significant were the ones requiring the Council to consider the introduction of certain parts of English civil law and the requirement to the Governor to follow the policy of the report of the Board of Trade of July 10, 1769. He was, on the one hand, to exercise very rigid control over the power of the Roman Catholic clergy and, on the other, to give every aid to the Church of England and even offer a cautious encouragement to such Canadian priests as might wish to break away from the discipline of their church.

7. You are forthwith to communicate such and so many of these Our Instructions to Our said Council, wherein their Advice and Consent are mentioned to be requisite . . .

8. You are to permit the Members of Our said Council to have and Enjoy Freedom of Debate and vote in all Affairs of Public Concern, that may be debated in Council.

12. . . . it will be the duty of the Legislative Council to consider . . . whether the Laws of England may not be, if not altogether, at least in part the Rule for the decision in all Cases of personal Actions grounded upon Debts, Promises, Contracts, and Agreements, whether of a Mercantile or other Nature; and also of Wrongs proper to be compensated in damages . . .

13. Security to personal Liberty is a fundamental Principle of Justice in all free Governments, and the making due provision for that purpose is an object the Legislature of Quebec ought never to lose Sight of; nor can they follow a better Example than that, which the Common Law of this Kingdom hath set in the Provision made for a Writ of Habeas Corpus, which is the Right of every British Subject in this Kingdom . . .[5]

20. The establishment of proper regulations in matters of ecclesiastical concern is an Object of very great importance, and it will be your indispensable duty to . . . give full satisfaction to Our new Subjects in every point, in which they have a right to any indulgence on that head; always remembering, that it is a toleration of the free exercise of the religion of the Church of Rome only, to which they are entitled, but not to the powers and privileges of it, as an established Church . . .

21. Upon these principles therefore, and to the end, that Our just Supremacy in all matters ecclesiastical, as well as civil, may have its due scope and influence, it is Our Will and Pleasure,—

First, that all Appeals to, or correspondence with any foreign ecclesiastical jurisdiction, of what nature or kind so ever, be absolutely forbidden under very severe Penalties.

Secondly, That no Episcopal or Vicarial Powers be exercised within Our said Province by any Person professing the Religion of the Church of Rome, but such only, as are essentially and indispensably necessary to the free exercise of the Romish Religion; and . . . not without a Licence and Permission from you . . . and under such . . . limitations . . . as may correspond with the spirit and provision of the Act . . . And no person whatever is to have holy Orders conferred upon him, or have the Cure of Souls without a License for the purpose first had or obtained from you.

Thirdly, That no person professing the Religion of the Church of Rome be allowed to fill any ecclesiastical Benefice . . . that is not a Canadian by birth, (such only excepted, as are now in possession of any such Benefice, . . .

Fourthly, That no person whatever, professing the Religion of the Church of Rome, be appointed Incumbent of any Parish, in which the Majority of the Inhabitants shall solicit the appointment of a Protestant Minister . . . But nevertheless the Roman Catholicks may have the use of the Church for the free exercise of their Religion at such time, as may not interfere with the Religious Worship of the Protestants . . .

Eighthly, That such Ecclesiasticks, as may think fit to enter into the holy state of Matrimony, shall be released from all Penalties, to which they may have been subjected in such Cases by any Authority of the See of Rome.[6]

d. The Act as Interpreted in Quebec.

Carleton, however, had already hinted while he was in London that he should exercise his own discretion in following his instructions on religious matters. He also seems to have decided to do the same thing in relation to the instructions requiring his Council to consider the introduction of certain parts of English law. As the communication of these instructions to the Council would imply that the Governor wished them to follow the suggestions of the home government, the failure to communicate them implied the reverse. From 1775, when Chief Justice Hey endeavoured to secure the acceptance by the Council of the "Plan of Judicature" referred to by Lord Dartmouth, until the departure of Carleton's successor, Haldimand, in 1784, the Governor steadily refused to give any encouragement to change. A number of the English officials united with the Canadian seigneurs to resist any change. Chief Justice Hey, although he had little respect for the political wisdom of the seigneurs, did hope to get his plan of judicature through the Council.

. . . The little I have seen of [the seigneurs] in Council gives me no Idea of their Abilities or moderation inflexible to any arguments either of expediency or justice they will admit no alteration in their

antient Laws particularly in the article of commerce which I insist
upon, & believe shall carry in favour of the English merchants, with
whom almost the whole trade of the country lyes . . .[7]

Hey was unsuccessful as we learn from the account of his successor,
Chief Justice Livius, who may be presumed to have had reliable
sources of information, including probably Hey himself.

> Such of the Canadian Seigneurs as were in the Council, knowing
> nothing of the King's pleasure but the Act, would hear of nothing
> but the strictest Canadian Law. 'Je me renferme dans le Bill' was
> the word with them. The Instructions would have levelled an oppo-
> sition that arose principally from respect to the King's supposed
> intentions; but in direct disobedience to his Instructions they were
> carefully concealed, and for want of them all was Contest and Con-
> fusion . . .[8]

Because of the American invasion the Council did not meet again
until early in 1777. Again Carleton failed to communicate his instructions on the matter of the law. At one point in the deliberations, when
he thought he had reason to fear that in spite of this lack of encouragement from the Governor the Council might pass an ordinance providing for jury trials in civil cases, he went so far as to intimate that he
would not give his consent to any such legislation.

Haldimand pursued a somewhat similar policy. Like Carleton, failing to communicate his instructions officially, he contrived to block
any legislative changes in the Council. By 1781, when repeated orders
from home compelled him to inform the Council officially of the wishes
of the home government, the official-seigneurial party was strong
enough to contain the mercantile opposition.

> . . . We are sensible that some alterations may and ought to be
> made in the laws and customs of Canada, but we apprehend that
> those should be made with moderation, and be more the effects of
> experience, than of any preconceived theory or opinion; and in the
> present critical state of the British Empire, it is with regret that we
> find ourselves obliged by our duty to the King to mention to Your
> Excellency the bad effects which the reports circulated every summer
> of changes to be made in the mode of administering the affairs of
> the province have upon his service. They disquiet the minds of the
> people, and furnish plausible pretences to the emissaries of the re-

volted colonies, and the other enemies of the state to insinuate that nothing is permanent under a British government; and the Quebec Act, the result of the generous and tolerating spirit which distinguishes an enlightened age and nation, was the effect of a narrow and interested policy, and would be repealed as soon as the ends for which it was made were effected.[9]

Members of the opposition did get their objections entered on the books of the Council as "reasons of protest."

. . . laws and customs of Canada which form the most imperfect system in the world, for a commercial people, have in matters of trade, been long since exploded in France and the Code-Marchande [sic] introduced into all their towns in its stead. Canada before the conquest of it by His Majesty's arms, had little or no trade of consequence, except that of the Indian Company for furs, who monopolized almost the whole, and therefore probably, not having so great occasion for the Code-Marchande or Jurisdiction-consulaire it was not introduced into this country.

The King's instruction points out a remedy to these notable inconveniences by amending the laws, restoring juries and the laws of England in all commercial affairs, leaving the custom of Canada to be the rule for decision of matters of landed property, of inheritance, and the like; and appointing the Chief Justice, the head of the law, to preside in the courts of common pleas, whose abilities, as a lawyer render him the fittest person to conduct the business of these courts . . .

The new system having hitherto been held forth to view with all its imperfections, without anything to soften, to correct, to reconcile with the wishes of the subject, has been an infinite prejudice to His Majesty's service. The Quebec Act is made *for vesting a limited legislative authority for a temporary period under many restrictions, and until it may be proper and expedient to call an assembly, and establish a full and complete legislature in the Province of Quebec*; it is therefore a matter of astonishment that gentlemen, in the very acts of legislation, should so far mistake or misconstrue that Act, as to assert that the report of changes to be made under so temporary a statute should disquiet the minds of the people, from apprehensions that nothing is permanent under a British government. A system *adopted* a law made only for a certain time *and under proper restrictions it being at that particular period inexpedient to call an assembly.* And therefore the very idea of an amendment of that law if it had not been held forth by the Act itself yet if circulated merely by reports, must produce very *contrary effects* on the minds of His Majesty's subjects, to those stated in the address.[10]

In 1784, after the war was over and legislation was at last passed guaranteeing the right of *habeas corpus,* the conservative party restated its position, using for the first time in reference to the Act, the word "charter" so often used later, but associating it oddly with a notion of total assimilation to the British people.

We the members of the Legislative Council humbly beg Your Excellency to take to the foot of the throne our strong and respectful gratitude for the gracious protection which His Majesty and the British nation have so generously granted to the peoples of this province during the unhappy disturbances which have affected a part of this continent; we attribute in great part the peace and other advantages which we have enjoyed during these unhappy times to the wisdom of the act of parliament passed in the 14th year of the present reign. We humbly beg Your Excellency to be kind enough to represent to His Majesty our sincere desire that this act should be continued in all its force; we wish nothing so much as to be able to transmit it to posterity as a precious charter which will ensure to the peoples of this province their enjoyment of their privileges and of their religion. We are convinced by experience and by the changes which have occurred since the conquest that Canadians will live happy by favour of this act and will in the not too distant future be indissolubly united (indissolublement incorporés) in the British nation. We venture to hope that Your Excellency will intercede to obtain for us this favour.[11]

Carleton and Haldimand had revealed to no one, and had failed to follow the instructions they received in relation to the Church. One of these, relating to the management of the seminaries, should have been communicated to the council because the Governor was supposed to associate himself with the Council in regulating these communities. All these instructions, however, remained a dead letter, Haldimand continuing Carleton's policy of trusting Bishop Briand, leaving him largely in control of the Church, and making no indiscreet inquiries about his connections with Rome. A letter addressed by Governor Haldimand to Lieutenant-Governor Hamilton on the occasion of his

departure from the province in the autumn of 1784 contains the only
reference which has been found to the non-observance by Carleton
and Haldimand of the instructions on religious matters. The copy
which has survived in the Colonial Office series is incomplete.

You will find amongst the royal instructions several relating to the
ecclesiastical affairs of the province; which in conformity to the
sentiments and conduct of my predecessors, I have thought could
not be carried into execution but with the greatest caution and
prudence, and in times of the most profound tranquility. I have
therefore not only allowed priests of the Roman Catholic religion
to remain amongst the Indians, but have encouraged the Seminary
St. Sulpice at Montreal to supply from their order missionaries
for the vacancies occasioned by the death of the Jesuits. I have likewise allowed the order of the Jesuits to remain upon the same foot-
ing that I found them, though I know that during the administration of Sir Guy Carleton, as well as my own, some of that order had
engaged in schemes and correspondence inconsistent with the allegiance and fidelity due to the King. You will find amongst the papers
extracts of letters . . . [subsequent page or pages are missing][12]

Two years later Chief Justice William Smith, the Loyalist, offered
a novel although not entirely new interpretation of the Quebec Act in
relation to the civil law.

The first cause I found in the Court or Appeals, raised the important Question, whether a subject of Controversy, in which the Parties
were English, as well as all who are interested under them, and no
Canadian concerned in the remotest Degree, called for a Decision
by the English or French Law? We reversed the Judgment of the
Common Pleas, which had in the most express Terms, held the
Doctrine, that the Quebec Act brought every Dispute of Property
without any exception, to the Test of the old Laws of the Colony
prior to the Conquest.
. . . I did not merely consent to the Reversal, but took up some
time in shewing, that in a case in which to do Justice, Resort must
be had to the French Code, *that Law* gave the Rule, and that the
Action and the Proceedings in it, ought to be in strict conformity to
the Quebec Act and the Provincial Ordinances; and where these
were silent, to the French forms of Practice, as far as the Modes
materially influenced the object and end of the Suit. And on the

other hand, that where the Cause was as purely English as the other was French, and Justice required a Reference to the English Law, *this Law* was the Test; and that if the same Statute and the Ordinances, did not authorize or justify a Deviation, the Practice of the Courts in England, directed the *main* Progress and conduct of the Suit.[13]

When Smith's decision was reported in London the law officers expressed surprise, but remarked cautiously that the only way to test the validity of his decision was to take a test case to the Court of Appeals in England.

Unhappily for historians the case was not tested. Smith's theory had been put forward in the province at least twice before by reputable lawyers. It seems astonishing to those who have familiarized themselves with the elaborate preliminary discussions and who are confident that they know the intention of the framers of the Act. Smith's position was, however, that theories as to intention cannot overturn the letter of the law. The careful reader of the article will notice that the wording will just bear Smith's interpretation. It may be significant that the corresponding clause in what is known as the "Third Draught of the Bill" is less ambiguous:

> . . . in all matters of controversy relative to Property and Civil Rights of any of His Majesty's Subjects *whether Canadian or English,* Resort shall be had to the Laws of Canada and *not to the Laws of England* for the Decision of the same, . . .[14]

Smith could not possibly have given his interpretation had this wording been retained. It is a matter for speculation whether he had noted the softened form of the enacting clause, and thought it deliberate.

NOTES

[1] *Journals of the Continental Congress*, Worthington Chauncey Ford, ed., Vol. I, pp. 87-8.

[2] S. & D., p. 660.

[3] *Ibid.*, pp. 670-71.

[4] S. & D., p. 585.

5 The King's Declaration of 1679 forbade arbitrary arrest in New France except for suspicion of treason or sedition. Thus, assuming that there was no right of Habeas Corpus in Quebec until one should be provided by ordinance, Canadians as well as English suffered a deprivation of liberty by the failure of the Governors to carry out this Instruction until 1784.

Habeas Corpus could be claimed under the common law, although judges could not be compelled to grant the writ. The power of arbitrary arrest was used cautiously by Haldimand; in practice, it was limited to the cases for which it had been permissible in New France, where there was a suspicion of sedition or treason.

6 S. & D., pp. 597-604.

7 S. & D., p. 671.

8 Colonial Office Papers (C.O.) 42, Vol. 9, pp. 118-19.

9 PAC, Quebec Legislative Council, Vol. D, pp. 77-8.

10 *Ibid.*, p. 83.

11 *Ibid.*, p. 178. Original in French. [Editor's translation.]

12 Haldimand to Lieutenant-Governor Hamilton, Nov. 14, 1784, C.O. 42, Vol. 47, p. 128.

13 S. & D., p. 841. For comments see L. S. F. Upton, ed., *Diary of William Smith* Vol. II, pp. xxv, 85, 95, 208-14. It should be noted, however, that the case cited by Upton as relevant originated before the passing of the Quebec Act, and that therefore the decision of the Appeal Court cannot well be cited in support of Smith's interpretation of the Quebec Act.

14 S. & D., p. 545. [Editor's italics]

PART 5

The Quebec Act: Secondary Works

1. LORD DURHAM

Durham was not a historian and the Durham Report was not a "history"; moreover the report does not even mention the Quebec Act specifically. Yet Durham's Report is the natural preface to a series of historical comments on the Quebec Act, for it was his brilliant persuasive and provocative Report which at once proclaimed and condemned the "French fact," and did so much to assure its survival. The recommendation of responsible government enabled moderate French Canadians peaceably to neutralize the purposes of those who framed the Act of Union; and the eloquence with which Lord Durham praised the Canadians (while pronouncing the inevitable extinction of the nation) provoked historians, French-Canadian and English-Canadian, into an increasingly scrupulous examination of the process of *la survivance*.

Lord Durham was an aristocrat of principles so liberal as to be deemed radical. On the continent a man of his views would ordinarily be associated with representatives of the many submerged peoples to whom national emancipation and the establishment of parliamentary government would go hand in hand. Durham, however, was less a Romantic than a man of the Enlightenment. He wanted good government as well as self-government, and he believed that the English and English institutions, including the monarchy, were peculiarly suited to provide both.

He was, moreover, naturally and rightly concerned with the relations of British North America to the United States and with the importance of preserving peace by making it obvious to the United States that the British colonies, free, secure and prosperous, were under no temptation to lend themselves to any plan of annexation. There seems to be no doubt that he gravely under-rated the grasp of constitutional principles and the political skill of the French-Canadian leaders, partly because he associated chiefly with their political opponents. The

French Canadians distrusted him and he did not know or understand them.

There was, however, another barrier. Durham, an aristocrat and land-owner, was also the traditional Whig, in close touch with the commercial and industrial interests of the nation. Much of his income, indeed, came from coal mines. His education, by private tutors, emphasized modern science and technology. His belief in nationalism was inseparable from an understanding of the economic basis of a viable national state. He looked forward to a Canadian nation formed from all the British North American colonies, united by modern technology, canals in central Canada, and railways everywhere. It is not surprising that he found the French Canadians, opponents of canals and public works of all kinds, taking little or no part in commerce or industry, and apparently content to extract a bare livelihood from their ill-managed farms, entirely unsuited to be the nucleus of the new British nation that should confront the American republic.[1]

Durham had in him, as Sir Charles Lucas says, along with liberal principles, something of a Stratford or a Cromwell It was natural to such a man to recommend the anticipation and the acceleration of what he saw was as an inevitable process of evolution.

There are two modes by which a government may deal with a conquered territory. The first course open to it is that of respecting the rights and nationality of the actual occupants; of recognizing the existing laws, and preserving established institutions; of giving no encouragement to the influx of the conquering people, and, without attempting any change in the elements of the community, merely incorporating the Province under the general authority of the central Government. The second is that of treating the conquered territory as one open to the conquerors, of encouraging their influx, of regarding the conquered race as entirely subordinate, and of endeavouring as speedily and as rapidly as possible to assimilate the character and institutions of its new subjects to those of the great body of its empire. In the case of an old and long settled country, in which the land is appropriated, in which little room is left for colonization, and in which the race of the actual occupants must continue to constitute the bulk of the future population of the province, policy as well as humanity render the well-being of the conquered people the first care of a just government, and recommend the adoption of the first-mentioned system; but in a new and unsettled country, a provident legislator would regard as his first object the interests not of the few individuals who happen at the moment to inhabit a portion of the soil, but those of that comparatively vast population by which he may reasonably expect that it will be filled; he would form his plans with a view of attracting and nourishing that future population, and he would therefore establish those institutions which would be most acceptable to the race by which he hoped to colonize the country. The course which I have described as best suited to an old and settled country, would have been impossible in the American continent, unless the conquering state meant to renounce the immediate use of the unsettled lands of the Province; and in this case such a course would have been additionally unadvisable, unless the British Government were prepared to abandon to the scanty population of French whom it found in Lower Canada, not merely the possession of the vast extent of rich soil which that Province contains, but also the mouth of the St. Lawrence, and all the facilities for trade which the entrance of that great river commands.

In the first regulations adopted by the British Government for the settlement of the Canadas, in the Proclamation of 1763, and the Commission of the Governor-in-Chief of the Province of Quebec, in the offers by which officers and soldiers of the British army, and settlers from the other North American Provinces, were tempted to accept grants of land in the Canadas, we perceive very clear indications of an intention of adopting the second and wiser of the two systems. Unfortunately, however, the conquest of Canada was almost immediately followed by the commencement of those discontents which ended in the independence of the United Provinces. From that period, the colonial policy of this country appears to have undergone a complete change. To prevent the further dismemberment of the Empire became the primary object with our statesmen; and an especial anxiety was exhibited to adopt every expedient which appeared calculated to prevent the remaining North American Colonies from following the example of successful revolt. Unfortunately the distinct national character of the French inhabitants of Canada, and their ancient hostility to the people of New England, presented the easiest and most obvious line of demarcation. To isolate the inhabitants of the British from those of the revolted Colonies, became the policy of the Government; and the nationality of the French Canadians was therefore cultivated, as a means of perpetual and entire separation from their neighbours.[2]

Thus, instead of availing itself of the means which the extent and nature of the Province afforded for the gradual introduction of such an English population into its various parts as might have easily placed the French in a minority, the Government deliberately constituted the French into a majority, and recognized and strengthened their distinct national character. Had the sounder policy of making the Province English, in all its institutions, been adopted from the first, and steadily persevered in, the French would probably have been speedily outnumbered, and the beneficial operation of the free institutions of England would never have been impeded by the animosities of origin.[3]

I will not here enter into the question of the effect of the mode of life and division of property among the French Canadians on the happiness of the people. I will admit, for the moment, that it is as productive of well-being as its admirers assert. But, be it good or bad, the period in which it is practicable, is past; for there is not enough unoccupied land left in that portion of the country in which English are not already settled, to admit of the present French population possessing farms sufficient to supply them with their present means of comfort, under their system of husbandry.[4]

. . . Were the French Canadians to be guarded from the influx of any other population, their condition in a few years would be similar to that of the poorest of the Irish peasantry.

There can hardly be conceived a nationality more destitute of all that can invigorate and elevate a people, than that which is exhibited by the descendants of the French in Lower Canada, owing to their retaining their peculiar language and manners. They are a people with no history, and no literature. The literature of England is written in a language which is not theirs; and the only literature which their language renders familiar to them, is that of a nation from which they have been separated by eighty years of foreign rule, and still more by those changes which the Revolution and its conquences have wrought in the whole political, moral and social state of France. Yet it is on a people whom recent history, manners and modes of thought, so entirely separate from them, that the French Canadians are wholly dependent for almost all the instruction and amusement derived from books: it is on this essentially foreign literature, which is conversant about events, opinions and habits of life, perfectly strange and unintelligible to them, that they are compelled to be dependent. Their newspapers are mostly written by natives of France, who have either come to try their fortunes in the Province, or been brought into it by the party leaders, in order to supply the dearth of literary talent available for the political press.[5]

In these circumstances, I should be indeed surprised if the more reflecting part of the French Canadians entertained at present any hope of continuing to preserve their nationality. Much as they struggle against it, it is obvious that the process of assimilation to English habits is already commencing. The English language is gaining ground, as the language of the rich and of the employers of labour naturally will. It appeared by some of the few returns, which had been received by the Commissioner of the Inquiry into the state of Education, that there are about ten times the number of French children in Quebec learning English, as compared with the English children who learn French. A considerable time must, of course, elapse before the change of a language can spread over a whole people; and justice and policy alike require, that while the people continue to use the French language, their Government should take no such means to force the English language upon them as would, in fact, deprive the great mass of the community of the protection of the laws. But, I repeat that the alteration of the character of the Province ought to be immediately entered on, and firmly, though cautiously, followed up; that in any plan, which may be adopted for the future management of Lower Canada, the first object ought to be that of making it an English Province; and that, with this end in view, the ascendancy should never again be placed in any hands but those of an English population.[6]

Students of Canadian history will be impressed at once by the remarkable understanding which Durham and his staff succeeded in gaining of the economic situation in Lower Canada during their relatively short stay in the province; and also by the great gaps in their information and interpretation which brought Durham to the surprising conclusion that the solid Canadian community on the St. Lawrence, united as it was by family ties, a common religion, common traditions and pride of ancestry, could quickly and easily have been assimilated by representatives of their former foes who did not even equal them in

numbers until nearly a century after the conquest. Durham's analysis
and the startling conclusions that he derived from it established the
ground over which historians have debated ever since.

2. POLITICAL HISTORIANS

a. François-Xavier Garneau[7]

François-Xavier Garneau came of a well-known Canadian family,
grew up in the city of Quebec in modest circumstances, was appren-
ticed to the notary Archibald Campbell in 1825, and became a reader
of literature, history and philosophy and an ardent admirer of Papineau. He developed his literary and political interests during a stay in
London and a visit to Paris. He returned to Quebec to give active
support to the reform movement. During the 1830's he contributed to
Le Canadien both poetry and prose. His interest was increasingly
drawn to the history of his own country, which since 1815 had been
attracting Michel Bibaud and a number of others. Garneau lived
through the anxious year of 1836, and the tragic events of 1837 and
1838; early in 1839 he must, with other intellectuals, have read
with interest, anger, and finally exasperation and disillusionment, the
long-expected Durham Report.

The Act of Union of 1840, with its direct attack on the French
language and its apparent hostility to the French Canadians, reinforced
by the administration of the unsympathetic Lord Sydenham, turned
Garneau more seriously to the task of vindicating his people against
what he believed to be unjust charges and injurious legislation. He did
not, however, take the easy way. Using his political influence to secure
a poorly paid government sinecure he devoted himself to steady and
serious study of the materials available to him in the archives of
Quebec. His first volume appeared in 1845—"the literary event of the
year and even of the epoch."

A pioneer work, written in these circumstances by the follower of
Papineau and of Lafontaine, and by the friend of Etienne Parent,
could not possibly be neutral.[8] It was without doubt Garneau's intention to be accurate and judicial, and he has generally been praised by
Canadian historians of both languages for his success in rising above
the political passions of the day. He wrote, however, as a liberal
nationalist of his day would be expected to write. He assumed that the

rights of stateless nations were a matter of moral law. He assumed that in 1764 as in 1840 Canadians thought of themselves as a nation and were consistent in demanding these rights. He also assumed, understandably in view of his recent political experiences, that Britain had been moved to do justice to the Canadians in 1774 only by the increasing disorders in the colonies to the south. He appears to have had access chiefly to official petitions and reports. He could not have had access to the correspondence of Murray or of Carleton.

The Petitions of the Canadians were welcomed, as they were bound to be in view of the current relations between Britain and the American colonies, and served as the basis of the Act of 1774, which itself was part of a much larger plan, which took into consideration all the English colonies on the continent. The increasing power of these colonies alarmed Britain more and more; their attitude since the peace [of 1763] is a sufficient explanation of the motives of Britain's policy toward Canada.[9]

The plans successively proposed for the government of Canada since 1763 have already been seen: the vain efforts to put some into execution, the investigations and the numerous reports presented by the principal officials of the colony, the Lords of Trade and Plantations and the law officers of the Crown; the requests of the colonists themselves, French and English, for a better government; and finally the claim of the English to exclude Roman Catholics from public office and from an elected assembly, a claim which was, as has been seen, the first cause of the antipathy between the two races in this country, and which only gave increased vigour to the French-Canadian nation. All these documents had been presented for the consideration of the Privy Council. From 1767 the House of Lords had declared that it was necessary to change the government of Canada in order to reform it, and make it more suited to the needs of the country. The Board of Trade had even summoned Carleton to help with his knowledge and experience in this difficult task. In 1764 the spirit of the government was completely hostile to the Canadians; by 1774 things had changed; its prejudices were now turned against the Americans and colonial assemblies. Interest triumphed over ignorance and passion. The permanent abolition of ancient institutions must inevitably have the effect of uniting Canadians with the discontented of the other colonies; this was understood, and conse-

quently the regulation of the Canadian question was delayed from
year to year until the authorities were obliged to act against Massa-
chusetts and the southern provinces. Thus the re-establishment of
French laws for long depended on the result of the attempt to tax
the colonies. The unconquerable opposition of the Americans helped
to persuade the ministry to listen to the remonstrances of the Canadians. Yielding to Canadian wishes served a double purpose; it at-
tached the clergy and nobility to the imperial cause, and it per-
suaded the people to recognize Britain's right to tax them; in the
opinion of Canadians this recognition was a small price to pay for
their preservation [as a people] and for the grant to them of political
privileges from which the English subjects madly wished to exclude
them.[10]

Garneau, with much persuasive logic, noted that from 1764 Britain
had been made aware of the wishes, and, as he would assume, the
natural rights of the Canadians. The fact that action came only when
the American crisis was becoming acute seemed to him to lead to a
simple and obvious conclusion. Britain was forced by fear and self-
interest to give in 1774 what in justice should have been given in 1764.
A number of historians have accepted this thesis. The fact that something like the policy of the Quebec Act was proposed and favoured
long before 1774 does not, of course, prove that the final resolution to
carry it out was not inspired by the revolutionary crisis.

It is easy to understand how Garneau came to the conclusion that
he did: he had insufficient knowledge of the political situation in Britain at this time; he entertained the current and over-simplified conception of the issues of the American Revolution; and he was not familiar
with some of the original sources which might have forced him to revise
his opinion of personal motives. When it is remembered that he had
seen Britain, as he supposed, stubbornly and unnecessarily refusing
redress of the grievances of the Assembly in Lower Canada until forced
into action by armed rebellion, and then responding with a determined
effort at anglicization, his judgment of the motives behind the Quebec
Act seems not only understandable, but inevitable.

The last few lines of the passage cited show that Garneau was not
aware of the great difficulty of knowing what "the people" wanted, or
whether they were in a position to define their wishes. He was a self-
taught historian, writing at a time when historical methodology was in

its infancy. It did not occur to him to think that he might know very little of the ideas and aspirations of his own people in the previous century.

There can be no question of the value of Garneau's magnificent pioneer work. It is, however, a useful exercise for the modern student to look over the short passage cited above and to ask how much of it may be based on evidence, how much unconsciously borrowed from the political rhetoric of the day, and how much may rest on that popular form of logic: "That's the way it must have been."

At the same time, reading this passage and others in Garneau's work may suggest to the student how important are contemporary events in stimulating the historian's imagination of the past and in suggesting to him the usefulness of a new approach to old material.

b. William Kingsford[11]

William Kingsford was the first English-Canadian historian to provide a lengthy continuous account of Canadian history from the time of Jacques Cartier to the death of Lord Sydenham. Untouched by the increasing racial and religious tensions in the Canada of his day, he reflects the gentle afternoon of Victorian optimism in his concluding words, "the progress of the Dominion has been steady and continuous. . . . British statesmen have not always acted wisely towards us; but there can be no doubt of the great truth that the mother country has increasingly desired our prosperity and happiness, and has made many sacrifices to sustain them. I believe that pride in this relationship is a dominant feeling in British North America."[12]

Military history plays a large part in Kingsford's narrative; of economic history, naturally, he is unaware. Although he had access to the Colonial Office correspondence and undoubtedly made some use of it, like Garneau he depended chiefly on official reports. Like Garneau, too, he was not fully aware of the complexities of the problem. Unlike Garneau he assumed that Canada was ruled by philosophers and statesmen whose concessions to French Canadians were inevitable even if somewhat regrettable. He took for granted the absolute value of liberal parliamentary institutions.

French Canada had left behind no political traditions. There was no trace of that personal liberty which, with all its imperfections, has been the vital principle of the British constitution. The system had been one of centralization, with the concentration of power in the persons of the governor and intendant. Neither the military nor civil administration extended any rights to the individual. There were only two active principles to which tradition could appeal: religion and the civil law, and both furnished in a certain measure their share of difficulty. The former, not in the matter of the personal profession of faith, but by the continuance of the laws to extend to the church recognized life, and to provide for the clergy the means of subsistence. The ancient law by its identification with the customs, habits, property, and protection from wrong and injury of all who remained under the new government, enforced the embarrassing duty of determining to what extent it should be maintained unchanged; or be modified, to be brought into harmony with British institutions. The proclamation of the treaty of peace was the commencement of the new system, by which personal liberty and progress were to be safeguarded: when differences of political thought were to be governed by law and reason; when the humblest of the new subjects was to be assured against arbitrary interference with his rights; when property was to be held sacred against spoliation, and when the field in which reward was attainable by merit, was to be thrown open to labour, enterprise, and probity.[13]

This passage shows the gulf that separates the present generation of Canadians from the late nineteenth century historian. Kingsford's knowledge of the institutions and customs of New France would be derived largely from the works of Francis Parkman. Kingsford seems, however, to have absorbed Parkman's general disapproval of the theory of absolutism rather than the ample information provided in the Parkman narrative which might be sufficient to make a reader question Kingsford's implication that "labour, enterprise, probity" and even "merit" found no recognition or reward in New France. The historian who confines himself to secondary works is inevitably in danger of exaggerating any false impression he may receive from them. The oratorical flourish at the conclusion of the foregoing passage reveals the profound complacency of even the intelligent English-speaking Canadian about British institutions at this time, a complacency which becomes understandable to one who reads the contemporary statements of the presumably unprejudiced Laurier on the same subject.

[The reports of the law officers] clearly prove the desire of the home ministry to lay the foundations of settled government in the province of Quebec, and extend to it fair and equitable liberty. They thus furnish a passage of history, to which we may turn with profit and satisfaction. The reply to any criticism, directed against the Quebec Act, lies in the query, What else could have been done? From the date when it was passed, being the period when the unfortunate Boston port act was carried through parliament, it has been to some extent the custom to adduce the influence of the disturbances, which at that date had reached their climax in the old provinces, as the main cause of the recognition of the ancient civil law of Canada, and the tolerance granted to the religion inherited by the people: as if the emergency had been viewed from the imperial standing point only. But I can discover no admissible ground for the acceptance of this belief. The act itself was the product of many years of enquiry and investigation: it is manifest throughout, that the first intellect available was directed to the consideration of the problem; and the result attained was based upon the desire only, of making good government in Canada possible, and of creating a loyal and satisfied population, with due respect to those imperial considerations, which it was not possible to disregard.[14]

I have dwelt at some length on the nine years of doubt and hesitation which intervened from the first consideration of a code of laws for the province, until the passage of the act, that, with the addition of English criminal law, accepted ancient civil law and custom in its entirety. I have been impelled to this course owing to what appears to me the incorrect assumption, or the misconception entertained regarding the act. It is still described by United States writers as designed to prevent the newly acquired province from joining with the other colonies. The facts I have stated prove the groundlessness of this pretension. No principle of law or justice suggested any other settlement of this difficult question. No alternative based on the nonacceptance of such considerations would have been acceptable. Possibly it is to be regretted that English procedure was not engrafted on that portion of civil law, which, in the view of most parties it was held wise to have retained.[15]

. . . I do not think it an extravagance to affirm, that the forms of French law being continued have aided in maintaining the French Canadian character unchanged, especially in the agricultural districts, and in preserving much as it was at the time of the conquest. The attempt to adhere to that tone of thought is still continued; many believe, more for the benefit of active politicians than for the French

Canadians themselves. Any innovation which has a tendency to dis-
integrate this sentiment is resisted; the conservative feeling with regard to the French civil law remains in all its strength, to preserve
the code without the least modification, as if a monument of super-
human wisdom.[16]

On the motives which prompted the Quebec Act, Kingsford comes
to a conclusion directly opposed to that of Garneau, and on equally
superficial evidence. Garneau assumes that Britain did justice only
when it was expedient to do so; Kingsford that Britain did in the end
do justice, and that, failing evidence to the contrary, nothing else was
ever intended or contemplated. The reader should consider carefully
Kingsford's explanation of the introduction of "the entire text of the
French civil law," asking himself (a) whether the Quebec Act did, in
fact, do this; (b) what dictated the precise wording that is used in the
Act; (c) what was the intent of the instructions that accompanied the
Act.

It may be assumed that Kingsford did not have access to the Dartmouth Papers. An examination of the Colonial Office Correspondence
that he did use suggests that he, like many other and greater historians,
was not able to make full use even of all the material available to him.
His strong British preferences, or prejudices, appear in his regretful
allusion to the tenacity of Canadian law.[17] It had not occurred to him
to consider that this law might have merits which the English law had
not; he could not forget the stain of despotism.

Kingsford's comment on the boundary clause shows the limitation of
his sources and of his understanding of the problem.

No one I think, can fairly deny that the act was wise and just in
its main provisions. One objection against it, in my humble opinion,
may be justly taken; the comprehension into the newly created province of the territory west of the settled parts of Canada at the period
of French rule. The act really enforced upon the inhabitants passing
into this territory the same laws which prevailed in Canada; and all
such immigration must have been from the British provinces. We
may safely assume that the British ministry considered that the time
had arrived, when a form of government should be given to the territory lately regained from the possession of hostile tribes, in the war
of 1763-1764. It had been then made available for settlement,
mainly through the bravery of imperial troops in the struggle which

had been so successfully terminated; and it was necessary to make some provision against its return to a state of lawlessness. It is possible, that the spirit of revolt dominant in the colonies may have led to the desire of preventing the exercise of any pretensions over this territory by the western provinces of Virginia and Pennsylvania; and of opposing by legislation all extension beyond their admitted frontier. If this theory be accepted, it furnishes an explanation of the incorporation of this western country into the jurisdiction of the province of Quebec, as constituted by the act.

The policy, whatever the motive, can only be regarded as exceedingly unwise. It caused great dissatisfaction: it effected no result. Canada should have been constituted a province from the eastern shores of the Saint Lawrence to its natural boundary and no further; to the island of Montreal including île Perrot. It was the limit of settlement. Beyond that locality, at the period of conquest, there was scarcely a white man established. Some straggling clearances had been made in the *seigneury* of Vaudreuil, but of such trifling importance as not to deserve consideration. On the southern shore Laprairie was the last settlement. No specific consideration, however, was called for south of the Saint Lawrence, owing to the limited amount of territory involved, the boundary line between Canada and New York, the forty-fifth parallel of latitude, striking the Saint Lawrence at lake Saint Francis.[18]

This passage is interesting evidence of the state of historical knowledge at the time at which Kingsford wrote. The economic historians had not begun to influence the writing of Canadian history and the pioneer work of C. W. Alvord on the political significance of the Ohio country was still in the future. Kingsford therefore writes two paragraphs of generalization on a subject that has since been illuminated by half a century of research.

c. Victor Coffin[19]

Among American historians, the tradition which associated the Quebec Act with "the intolerable acts" remained throughout the nineteenth century, while Canadians like Goldwin Smith, in their disapproval of the French Canadian fact and of the policy that had permitted it, were as emphatic as Durham and historically less reliable.[20] In 1896 there was an important advance. Victor Coffin produced, as a doctoral thesis for the University at Madison, a detailed and well-documented monograph on the Quebec Act in its historical setting. No historian before him and none after, until A. L. Burt, made such a full examination of the relevant sources.

Although agreeing with Durham and Goldwin Smith that the results of the Quebec Act were lamentable, Coffin undertook to prove beyond all question the casual assumption of Kingsford that the act was intended not to punish the colonies but to give an appropriate government to Quebec—"the main desire of the authors of the measure was to further the security and prosperity of the Province and fulfill treaty obligations toward the French Canadians."[21] Coffin admits that the boundary clause in particular angered the colonies, but he looks upon it as the reasoned continuation of an established British policy against inland settlements.

Coffin therefore acquits Great Britain of having intended to use the Quebec Act for the coercion of the American colonies. He does, however, condemn the Act as strongly as, or more strongly than Lord Durham had done.

> . . . the Quebec Act is really one of the most unwise and disastrous measures in English colonial history. It will be shown below that it was founded on the misconceptions and false information of the Provincial officials; that though it secured the loyal support of those classes in Canada,—the clergy and the noblesse,—whose influence has been represented as all important, at the critical juncture this proved a matter of small moment. For the noblesse were found to have no influence, and that of the clergy was found in main measure paralyzed by the provision which had again laid on the people the burden of compulsory tithes. Without the Act the old ruling classes, there is every reason to believe, would have taken precisely the same attitude, and the people would not have been exposed to those influences which ranged them on the side of the invader. Apart from Canadian affairs, the disastrous effect of the measure on public feeling in the older provinces must be strongly considered in any estimate as to its expediency.[22]

Here Coffin does a good deal of guessing. Chief Justice Hey certainly accused Carleton of having "taken an ill measure of the influence of the seigneurs and Clergy over the lower order of the people"[23] and Carleton almost acknowledged that he had been over-optimistic,[24] but the evidence of neither gives any support to Coffin's assumption that a totally contrary policy could have been followed successfully. No evidence has been found to support Coffin's statement that the influence of the clergy was largely "paralyzed by the provision . . . of compulsory tithes," although it was not sufficient to prevent Canadians in areas affected by the invasion from cooperating more or less willingly with the invader.

Coffin clears the ministry of ulterior motives on the difficult matter of the extension of the boundary in such fashion as to include in the new province the whole of the Ohio territory. He devotes over thirty pages to an examination of British policy in relation to the western lands, anticipating later writers in showing that from 1760 on nothing in the correspondence or memoranda on western lands gives evidence of any developing hostility on the part of Britain toward the colonies, but that, on the contrary, there was a consistent development of the policy that might be expected from a commercial monopolist empire, and a natural desire to prevent hostilities with the Indians. Moreover, the policy, he says, was dictated "neither by the acquisition of Canada nor by the colonial troubles of the seventies." It was only a new application of that principle of commercial monopoly which runs through twenty-nine acts "from the year 1660 to the unfortunate period of 1764."[25] He goes on, however:

But while defending the originators of the Quebec Act from the heavier reproach brought against them on this point, I do not wish to be understood as in the least defending the Western policy of the measure in itself. Disastrous as the Quebec Act proved, no part of it I think was more shortsighted or more disastrous than this treatment of the Western lands. Following up the Proclamation of 1763, it seemed an attempt to indefinitely maintain in the great heart of the continent, when apparently thrown open for Anglo-American expansion, the policy of monopoly and restriction against which the colonies on the coast were chafing so sorely. It was natural that the latter should imagine themselves threatened and impeded more malignly and seriously than could have proven to be the case; it was on this side, I have little doubt, that the Quebec Act figured most prominently amongst the colonial grievances. Great Britain might well seem to have become "the most active foe of the English race in America." In this light I am inclined to emphasize strongly the importance of the Act in alarming and embittering the colonists.[26]

Coffin thus anticipates most later historians in dissociating the Quebec Act firmly from the "intolerable acts."

Coffin also breaks new ground in his insistence that the Act be understood in light of the instructions to the governor as to the policy to be pursued, and even in the light of the preceding debates in the House of Commons. His comment on the religious provisions is interesting and finds no echo in the work of any historian until the 1960's. By treating the instructions as an effective part of the general legislative policy he comes near to maintaining that the Act may be seen as almost hostile to the Roman Catholic Church.

The prominence of the religious element in Canada, and the position the Roman Catholic Church had so long occupied in secular matters as well, made the treatment of that church, and its future position, one of the most important and pressing of the problems that confronted the new Government. The conquerors were pledged by the Capitulation to full toleration of the Roman Catholic worship; though that instrument, promising to all religious communities the continued enjoyment of their property, had distinctly refused to assure the tithes or other dues of the secular clergy.[27]

It [is] very doubtful if the position of the Church was really much improved by the enactment, supposing the latter to be rigidly applied .... There were new elements indeed of positive disadvantage. The clergy were now legally assured of support; but that support, we are frequently told, had been, since the conquest, quite as assured by the voluntary contributions of a pious people, over the recalcitrant of whom might still be exercised, in the generally hazy state of the ecclesiastical powers, a great share of the many-sided authority so abundantly wielded under the old régime. Now however the Quebec Act had strictly and narrowly defined the real position and power of the Church; it had stripped it of nearly every vestige of its old temporal prestige, and of every right of pretension to any but a strictly religious status. Further, this Act had in all probability actually diminished the revenues of the Church; for it had deprived it entirely not only of all right to dues from benefices unfilled, (and the filling of vacancies was in the hands of a Government ordered to lose no opportunity of securing the advancement of the Protestant religion, to whose benefit the receipts from such vacancies were to be appropriated), but also of all right to dues from any parish in which a majority of Protestants might become settled. It must therefore appear that the apprehensions of the Continental Congress as to the establishment of the Popish worship were unfounded; that the position and prospects of the Church through the new legislation, especially when viewed in that connection with the previous policy and the accompanying instructions which shows its intent and the spirit in which it would be administered, were not such as to give evidence of an exceptional liberality which could be explained only by sinister designs against the other colonies.[28]

A reading of the instructions on religious matters confirms what Coffin has said, although his assertion that the enforcement of tithes was of no special advantage to the Church is hardly consistent with his previous statement that it was this same provision which inspired the hostility of the habitants to the Act.[29] He is, of course, quite right in arguing that the illiberality of the instructions refutes the suggestion that Britain was motivated in this matter by hostility to the other colonies. He failed to note that the instructions were, and remained, apparently with the good will of the British government, a dead letter. Inevitably, this gives a misleading impression of the impact of the Act and perhaps even of the intentions of its framers.

Coffin also shows that the provisions concerning the civil law in the Act appear very different when they are seen in the light of the instructions.

That the profession of an intent of bringing in English law through Provincial enactment was sincere was shown by the action supplementary to the Quebec Act. In the Instructions to Carleton in 1775 for his guidance, especially in future legislation, he is enjoined by the 12th Art. [There follows a summary of Article 12, see p. 60] Viewed in connection with the 13th Art., which recommends the taking of measures to secure to the Province the benefits of the principle of Habeas Corpus, this shows that the administration cannot be justly accused of being willing that the Government should revert entirely to the old principles and forms. It is apparently intended rather that only so much of the old law should be retained as could in any way be contended for as essentially bound up with the securing to the French Canadians that full enjoyment of their property which had been promised in the Capitulation and Treaty. That this limit was not adhered to was due in part to a necessary development of what was now done; in part to the confirming and extending of the main policy of the Quebec Act during and after the revolutionary war.[30]

In relation to the law it will be noted that Coffin does mention that the policy of the Act as seen in the instructions was not carried out. He goes on to argue that the assumption of hostile critics that the Quebec Act was intended to introduce a despotic form of colonial government in that it denied an assembly is unfair because, as he says correctly, the Act intimated that an assembly was deferred rather than denied. He supports this argument by quoting from Lord North, who, in the debates on the Act, emphasized that the arrangement was not intended to be "perpetual," and he suggests that it was not to be expected that the administration would be content to govern the colony for very long by a legislature with no power of direct taxation. He makes a remark which perhaps should be pondered by those who are inclined to read too much into the Quebec Act. "In fact the action taken in this particular must simply be looked upon as the shelving of a difficult subject,—as a continuation of a policy of delay and compromise which had marked all previous dealings with Canada."[31]

Coffin concludes this part of his discussion by presenting a piece of evidence which, if negative, is still convincing.

With regard then to the origins of the Quebec Act it need only be added that the above examination must at least show that if that Act were in any important degree due to the causes assigned it by colonial suspicion, the government which originated and pushed it through must have taken unusual pains to keep its reasons and its purposes hidden. But why should such concealment have been thought necessary with regard to the whole or any part of the enactment? This same government has just carried through three Bills of the most stringent and repressive nature, striking, to the popular view, heavier blows at American freedom and growth than anything contained in the Quebec Act, and had found itself in these measures backed by a consistent and overwhelming support, both in Parliament and throughout the country. Why should it now have scrupled to say that it was also taking measures of precaution in Canada? The government of that day was not an enlightened one, and would have been content to secure popular support, without looking to the future; it might well have concluded, for example, that the preserving of the vast regions of the West from the encroachments of the rebellious colonies would prove a popular measure. Rather than concealed indeed, we might expect to see this motive, if occupying a prominent position in the Government mind, put forward with prominence. We might expect to find it used to explain and defend the more doubtful parts of the measure, and especially that apparent establishing of the Roman Catholic Church which so aroused the horror of the Continental Congress, and which was almost as unpopular in England as in America. On the other hand, if the *secret* design hinted at by the opposition and believed in by the colonists had existed, it is not to be supposed that it would [not] have been alluded to by such able and prominent members of the party as Wedderbourne and Lyttleton.[32]

Coffin's exhaustive treatment of the motives of the Quebec Act is so complete and convincing that it is surprising that so little acknowledgement has been made of his work by historians like A. L. Burt who have come to substantially the same conclusions. He also touches on another matter neglected by most other historians, the importance of bearing in mind, in making moral judgments, the moral principles of the age being judged. Coffin is convinced that the Quebec Act was unnecessary in its provisions and disastrous in its results. He therefore takes issue strongly with those who argue that it was a concession to the moral rights of the Canadians, pointing out that the principles of the eighteenth century by which the actions of eighteenth century statesmen must in great measure be judged did not attach a sacred character to nationality.

. . . What else could have been done, we are asked,—usually with extravagant laudation of the humanity and generosity of the British government in thus pursuing the only path open to it. It has been one of my objects to try and show that something else, something very different, *could* have been done . . . that the alternative course was simply to set the new English Province firmly and definitively upon an *English* instead of a *French* path of development. As shown above, the way was clearly pointed out by other advisers as well qualified to speak as those whose advice was taken in 1774. I know that in this our age of highly-defined and all-pervading nationality, this apparently light hearted and reckless treading upon the holy ground of national development may bring down upon me the severest censures. But my critics will remember that we are dealing with another age, one in which nationality was not the breath of the political nostril; one in which new and alien acquisitions were absorbed and assimilated as an every day process. . . .

In the discussions in Parliament and out with regard to that measure, both before and after its enactment, we find that its advocates insist with strong self-righteousness that in Canada it is the French

Canadian only who is to be considered; that the small English section there has scarcely a right to be heard; that Canada (as Carleton
had urged), was French and destined to remain French; that it was
probably for the interest of Great Britain to discountenance any
large English admixture. This view I have shown above was no doubt
largely due to the incorrect ideas which Murray and Carleton had
fostered with regard to the origin and character of the English already in the Province.[33]

Coffin goes on to argue, without offering evidence, that the assimilation of the Canadians to English ways was practicable and would have
been desirable. Few historians today could be found to agree with him
on this matter. Carefully as he has sifted some of the evidence in relation to the Act, it is impossible to avoid the conclusion that here his
beliefs are based on his wishes. It must be remembered that his study
was limited, a monograph on the Quebec Act and its immediate after-
math. Had he been more familiar with the later history of Canada and
the later development of the French-speaking community he would
probably not have been prepared to say that a single piece of legislation was sufficient to change the whole character of a nation. Near the
close of his discussion he quotes Lord Durham with approval: "The
system of government pursued in Lower Canada has been based on the
policy of perpetuating that very separation of the races . . . which it
ought to have been the first and chief care of Government to check and
extinguish." Like Durham, he assumes (and without offering any satisfactory evidence) that extinction was possible.

d. Adam Shortt[34]

Adam Shortt, one of the great pioneers in Canadian historical research, with a special knowledge of the period of the Quebec Act
(A. Shortt and A. G. Doughty: *Documents . . . 1760-1791*), published what can only be termed a somewhat harsh review of Coffin's
work. He begins by faint praise for the author's lack of bias, but then
goes on to a rebuke which is so peevish in tone as to suggest that it might
even be inspired by unconscious jealousy. Shortt takes issue with Coffin
chiefly on his treatment of the motives of the Quebec Act. He argues
that the policy of the Quebec Act cannot possibly be isolated from the
general situation in North America, the rebellious tendencies of the
colonies, and particularly the danger of French intervention. The Quebec Act, he maintains, represented the policy of Carleton, a novice at

administration but an able, experienced military officer. Shortt depends on Carleton's despatches in the year 1767-68 to show that his policy, accepted by the British government, was conceived with the potentially rebellious colonies constantly in mind. After an extensive examination of the general situation in Quebec and Carleton's views on it, he concludes,

> . . . Carleton thought that if Canada were placed once more upon a French basis, and its limits extended so as to include the western Indians, not only would the old colonies to the south be prevented from extending further to the west, and thus getting beyond the control of the mother country; if they presumed to carry their present pretensions to freedom and insubordination any further, England would have at her disposal in Canada that joint power of the Frenchman and the Indian which had been the great terror of the colonists. It was this that had kept them so closely dependent upon Britain during the whole of their previous history, and the relief from this fear, by the conquest of Canada, was coincident with the rise of their present most ungrateful and rebellious claims. Such was the attitude of Carleton, a man at this time of no experience or capacity as a civil governor, but an experienced and far-sighted military officer, and such was his view of the policy to be adopted in the government of Canada. This policy he finally managed to impress upon the British Government, and it was his view which prevailed in the framing of the Quebec Act. Of this there is abundant evidence, both throughout the documents of the period in the Canadian Archives and in the literature of the time dealing with this question, though, from the nature of the subject, it was not very openly alluded to by either the Government or its opponents.[35]

The power of an influential reviewer is shown by the apparently devastating effect of Shortt's comments on Coffin's reputation:

> Coffin's *Province of Quebec and the American Revolution* a volume prepared from the new material in the Canadian Archives with all the apparatus of recent scholarship, was reviewed by Adam Shortt with such effect that Shortt's devastating twelve-page review (it is safe to say) has supplanted the original in the texture of Canadian history. Pope's volume of Confederation Documents was reviewed by Sir John Bourinet in terms more scathing, perhaps, if not quite so permanent in their evaluation.[36]

This may be an overstatement, but it may also explain in part why Coffin's impressive pioneer study has not received more attention from Canadian historians. The reader of Carleton's letters will agree that they do show a constant preoccupation with defence, and that defence is seen in terms of new civil arrangements as well as of special military measures. On the other hand Coffin does not deny that Britain was aware of the dangers from Boston and Virginia, and he admits that the Act antagonized the colonies. His main contention is that the Act was passed for Quebec rather than against the American colonies. Shortt's only answer to this is his insistence that the Act was Carleton's, and that Carleton was thinking chiefly of the Americans—and the letters give considerable if not complete support for this view. Shortt, however, rounds out his case by emphasizing the military factor of the Indians in the general design. For this there is no support in Carleton's letters. Indians were used in the American Revolutionary War, but not by Carleton (except for scouting purposes). It was well known that Carleton, conspicuously humane in warfare, was most reluctant to employ Indians who, uncontrolled, would use their own methods. Shortt seems here to yield to the common temptation to make a good case better by apparently impressive but unsubstantiated statements.

e. John G. Bourinot[37]

An extract from Bourinot's brief work is given here chiefly because he is perhaps the first historian to use the expression of the seigneurial party of 1784 in speaking of the Act as "the charter" of French Canadians. Bourinot, like Kingsford, assumes that the authors of the Act had no motives beyond their professed one of making better provision for the government of the province.

> A close study of official documents from 1764 until 1774 goes to show that all this while the British government was influenced by an anxious desire to show every justice to French Canada, and to adopt a system of government most conducive to its best interests ... Attorney-General Yorke and Solicitor-General De Grey in 1766 severely condemned any system that would permanently "impose new, unnecessary and arbitrary rules (especially as to titles of land, and the mode of descent, alienation and settlement), which would tend to confound and subvert rights instead of supporting them." In 1772 and 1773 Attorney-General Thurlow and Solicitor-General

Wedderbourne dwelt on the necessity of dealing on principles of justice with the province of Quebec. The French Canadians, said the former, "seem to have been strictly entitled by the *jus gentium* to their property, as they possessed it upon the capitulation and treaty of peace, together with all its qualities and incidents by tenure or otherwise." . . . The result of the deliberation of years was the passage through the British Parliament of the measure known as "The Quebec Act," which has always been considered the charter of the special privileges which the French Canadians have enjoyed ever since, and which, in the course of a century, made their province one of the most influential sections of British North America.[38]

Bourinot, as the passage suggests, confined himself largely to the reports of the law officers and assumed that they were the guide used by the government in determining its policy. This has been questioned by many historians who rely partly on the evidence of William Knox, Under Secretary of State for the Colonies.[39] The contrast here between Shortt and Bourinot is striking, even amusing. For his particular purpose each man uses his own set of documents and appears to ignore those of the other.

f. Duncan McArthur[40]

In spite of his severity toward Coffin, Adam Shortt, in his capacity of editor-in-chief of the ambitious *Canada and Its Provinces*, a twenty-two volume survey of the whole of Canadian history, allowed Duncan McArthur to present an essay on the Quebec Act very much slighter and less well-documented than Coffin's although McArthur had available to him the resources of the Public Archives and the recently published collection of *Documents* by Shortt and Doughty.

McArthur was an Ontarian, a professor at Queen's University in the Laurier period and after. Striving to be "liberal," repudiating bigotry, repudiating any anti-French sentiment, asserting the values of French-Canadian nationalism, although clearly not very happy about it, McArthur goes even beyond Garneau in attributing the Quebec Act to the American situation. He finds its chief merit in the religious clauses; had he read the Act more carefully and associated it with the accompanying instructions, his comments on both religious and legal clauses might have been modified. Coffin's discussion was available to him but he made no use of it, although his general conclusion that the Act was a mistake is the same as Coffin's. As is perhaps understandable in a work written in part for the intelligent general reader, he spends rather more time on the consequences, which are speculative, than on the causes which, to some extent, are ascertainable.

> The Quebec Act manifests a complete change in the attitude of the British government towards Canada. . . . North, Hillsborough, Germain and the second-rate statesmen who directed British policy thought they saw in the conquest of Canada one of the most potent causes of American disaffection. . . .
> The object of the Quebec Act was twofold. It was designed, in the first place, to retain the loyalty of French Canada. But it expressed a deeper and more subtle purpose. By intrenching the French-Canadian race on the St Lawrence and by extending French-Canadian dominance to the vast hinterland, it was hoped to break and dispel the force of the rising wave of independence in the southern colonies. The Quebec Act was formed with an eye fixed, not on Quebec, but on Boston.[41]

McArthur here borrows and somewhat extends Shortt's theory on the motives of the Quebec Act, ignoring all opposing evidence and indeed not troubling to refer to evidence in support of his thesis. His reference to the British statesmen shows also the somewhat superficial nature of his work. North, as Prime Minister, and Hillsborough, as former President of the Board of Trade, made representations on the Quebec Act, but Germain was not involved and the man chiefly responsible, Dartmouth, the Colonial Secretary, is not even mentioned.

McArthur finds the Quebec Act a partial failure both in its immediate and its more remote results.

> . . . during the ten years of British civil government—through no fault of theirs—both clergy and noblesse had lost their grip on the mass of the people. The authority of government, under British administration, was weakened. The habitant was given a taste of freedom, and the authority both of priest and of seigneur began to appear in the light of an unnecessary restraint. The French Canadians of this class—and they were numerous—remained loyal, not because of the Quebec Act, but in spite of it. In its more immediate

purpose the Quebec Act was therefore only moderately successful. On the other hand, in its ulterior purpose the Quebec Act was a dismal failure; for the New England colonies were not intimidated by the presence of a French nation on the banks of the St Lawrence. . . . The United States of America is the witness to the failure of this, the real purpose of the Quebec Act.[42]

McArthur gives a good deal of attention to the remote results of the Quebec Act. Taking the provisions of the Act separately, he argues, but without evidence, that before 1774 a new Canadian law, both French and English, was being formed by the ordinances of the Governor and Council. This again is a sample of stating as a fact what might have been or perhaps must have been. There is no real evidence for any such statement and, as has been shown, there are grave doubts whether any of the legislation passed was valid. He goes on to praise the provision for the recognition of the Roman Catholic religion because "religion is one of the fundamental interests of the human being" and "has been the chief concern of [the French Canadians'] daily life." Also, "the clergy was made the ally of the government" and "the weight of the church was to be found exerted on behalf of the crown and the British connection." More than this, McArthur notes that with the coming of the Loyalists there might have been not only much religious prejudice but even a religious civil war, had not the British government, although moved by other motives, "removed from the petty sphere of Canadian politics the question of the status of the Roman Catholic Church in the Province of Quebec".

For these advantages however, McArthur argues, the price was heavy. He attacks the whole law, perpetuated as he says by the Quebec Act as "an impediment to commercial progress and harmonious intercourse between the races":

This body of civil law was of such a complicated character that even French lawyers disagreed in its interpretation. When it became necessary to introduce a popular assembly, French and English became arrayed on opposing sides on issues arising out of the interpretation of the civil code. This situation welded the French-Canadian race into a party and was responsible for the complications of 1837. Likewise, the granting by a single act of all the guarantees of French-Canadian nationalism placed nationalism—by nature none too tolerant—completely beyond the sphere of compromise. No further concessions could be made, and consequently the spirit of compromise—so necessary to the welfare of the two Canadian races—was robbed of its means of support.[43]

McArthur concludes with a repetition of the cliché that the Quebec Act was a "charter of liberties." He admits, as Coffin does not, that the French-Canadian nationality could not have been submerged. He then goes on rather awkwardly in the face of his previous comments to say:

.... The destruction of French-Canadian nationalism, had it been possible, would have been a national calamity. Nationalism has created its problems and will do so in the future, but it contributes to the wealth of the Canadian people an element which simply cannot be estimated. French-Canadian nationality is one of Canada's greatest assets, and for its preservation the credit belongs largely to the church of Quebec. But for the development of French-Canadian nationalism as an uncompromising political creed, with its instinctive tendency towards separation and isolation, the responsibility rests with the Quebec Act of 1774.[44]

McArthur might have been ignored had his work not been the only brief and presumably reliable narrative available to English-speaking readers before the publication of Coupland's *The Quebec Act*. Considering the material available, McArthur's work seems less thorough than that of Garneau seventy-five years before. After a superficial survey of sources he made a judgment dictated, as might be expected, largely by his own view of the current social and political scene. This is popular history and useful in its way, catering to a very general desire that history be applicable to present day concerns, that it be obviously and clearly "relevant." The danger of this approach to scholarly history is clear. There is a strong temptation to select and arrange available material in such a way as to fit one's conceptions of the current situation, its problems and its needs. It is all too easy with one's mind fixed on the present to slip into generalizations partly or wholly inaccurate. For example, an examination of the doings of the Legislative Assembly in Lower Canada from 1792 to 1836 certainly does not bear out McArthur's suggestion that the chief issue between French and English was the interpretation of the civil code, or that it was principally defence of the code as such that "welded the French-Canadian race into a party." McArthur's essay as a whole is interesting and stimulating but it cannot be called scholarly.

g. Thomas Chapais[45]

Thomas Chapais' treatment of the Quebec Act suggests that, like his contemporary Laurier, he was a loyal French Canadian and also an admirer of the British Liberal tradition. His book is based on lectures given at Laval University. He appears to have made a diligent use of the printed sources, the works of Francis Maseres, the *Constitutional Documents* of Shortt and Doughty, the Cavendish *Debates*, and also the unprinted C. O. 42 ("Q") series available in transcript at the Public Archives. As he says himself (pp. 169-70, n. 1) he did not read Victor Coffin's book until his own was completed, but (as the passage cited below shows) he came to the same conclusion as Coffin on the origins of the Act.

A more careful reading of the *Constitutional Documents* and especially of the Instructions accompanying the Quebec Act might have caused him to be more restrained in his praise. Although more thorough and much more precise in citing sources, he resembles McArthur in a preoccupation with results. McArthur will not condemn the general religious toleration of the Quebec Act, but, disliking some of the consequences, he attacks the method and the motive. Chapais, seeing the Act as a "charter" and the foundation of subsequent national growth, is generous in his praise of those who, imperfect though they might be, followed as he believed the most enlightened and liberal principles. The economic aspects of the measure do not interest him. The significant and contentious boundary clause is dismissed in a few lines as "important for the future but scarcely affecting the graver problems of the day *(du présent)* (pp. 165-66). Even on these graver problems his conclusions may seem to the critical student too simple, and perhaps too benevolent.

> [The Quebec Act] marked a critical point, a point of ascent along the new path in which the mysterious decrees of Providence were directing our destiny. To a régime of uncertainty and of personal rule, there succeeded a régime of familiar law and order. We emerged from our vague condition to assume definite status. We were freed from a precarious toleration and were put in possession of a legal guarantee. For the last ten years we had been struggling against a group, few in numbers but arrogant, who claimed to dominate us by excluding us in virtue of their conquest. Arbitrating between this group, English in race and Protestant in faith, and us, French in race and Catholic in faith, the English Parliament, whatever may have

been its motives and its plan, decreed in our favour and proclaimed our rights. For the first time since 1760, it determined by legislation our government and our institutions. And this first act of imperial legislation decreed at the same time in a large measure our religious emancipation and our national emancipation. This was a fact of tremendous importance which was to be fruitful in happy results. The Quebec Act was perhaps more important for what it implied than for what it decreed. For us it suppressed the Oath of Supremacy; and this necessarily meant that Catholicism was fully recognized and on an equality with official Protestantism. It granted to the priests the legal right to collect the tithe; and that for good and ill meant that the Catholic Church was recognized in Canada by the British state. It re-established incontestably our old French civil law, because it was better adapted to our outlook, to our principles, our customs and our traditions; this inevitably involved the acknowledged survival of these traditions, customs, manners, and this outlook, the essential elements of our French nationality. Yes, all that potentially was in the Quebec Act! From June 22, 1774 we had a British charter that we could invoke, on which we could depend, and which preserved a base for our future claims.[46]

Chapais goes on to repudiate the association of the Quebec Act with the intolerable acts, which he refers to as "a current and generally accepted opinion." His theory is that Carleton "occasionally used the American argument to support his recommendations. But he had other arguments too . . ." and he gives Carleton great praise for his achievement.

The passage quoted, however, shows again the danger of a preoccupation with results. It is true that Chapais gives an invaluable, imaginative insight into the possible impact of the Quebec Act (apart from particular clauses) when he refers to the fact that it gave to the French-Canadian Roman Catholics a "definite status," freed them from "a precarious toleration" and put them in possession of a "legal guarantee." It is very likely that this was, if not at the time, at least later, the psychological effect of the Quebec Act on some Canadians, although as will be shown, evidence is largely wanting. Unfortunately Chapais elaborates this theme and goes on to make entirely inaccurate statements. The Quebec Act did substitute a special oath to be taken by French-Canadian officials for the usual oath of supremacy but this certainly did not mean that Catholicism was "fully recognized" and "on an equality with official Protestantism." The instructions accompanying the Act show the very reverse. The Church did in practice achieve something like equality, but only through the special circumstances of war and the special cooperation of Carleton, Haldimand and their successors. Moreover, the Quebec Act could hardly be said to re-establish "incontestably" the old French civil law. The Act provided a legislature to amend the law and both the debates before the Act and the instructions which accompanied it indicated that it was the intention of the authorities that the law should be amended. Chapais again uses the word "charter" in the sense that it had been used about the time of the Quebec Act as a gift of law from the King to his people, and a guarantee that the law would not henceforth be altered. This was the seigneurial interpretation of the Act, but there is no evidence for reading it into the policy of the Act.

h. Lionel Groulx[47]

The abbé Lionel Groulx, a younger contemporary of Chapais, who lectured in history at the University of Montreal, was a much more ardent and less liberal nationalist. He read and wrote history with his heart and soul, as well as with his mind. He had been profoundly influenced by the events which marked the end of the Laurier era and the years of the First World War: the prolonged efforts of Laurier, during a period of international tension and the pressure of the imperial federation movement, to hold the balance between English and French-speaking Canadians, the prolonged struggle over separate schools in Manitoba in the 1890's, and over the teaching of French in Ontario in the years before 1914. His publications span a period of over 60 years, (1906-1967). He wrote on various themes relating to French-Canadian nationalism, but from the time he began to lecture at the University of Montreal he wrote increasingly on the history of his people. Many of his lecture series were published (*Nos luttes constitutionnelles*, 1915-16, *La Confédération Canadienne, ses origines*, 1918, etc). In 1926 appeared *Vers L'Emancipation* from which the following comment on the Quebec Act is taken. L'Abbé Groulx's viewpoint is perhaps best expressed by himself in the introduction to this volume. Having insisted that his lectures are only "essais" he continues:

We are convinced that we have spared neither time nor research in order to make our investigation as complete as possible. One who calls himself an historian does not stress his own integrity.

Independence of mind becomes difficult and dangerous to the French-Canadian historian who undertakes to judge the English conquest and English methods of governing the conquered. *Ce n'est plus d'être indulgent qu'on lui sait mauvais gré, c'est d'être juste. Les hommes souffrent malaisément qu'on applique aux puissants les règles de la morale commune.*

We shall explain the matter at greater length in this volume; we do not confuse impartiality with neutrality. History is a moral act, and consequently not independent of ultimate values (*finalités suprêmes*). Our ambition and our right are to write and to teach it as a Catholic and a French-Canadian is bound to do. The historian must work and think with his whole personality; if he becomes neutral and indifferent we must say with Bossuet "he abdicates the quality of a man."[48]

Groulx argues at great length from the letters of Carleton written from Quebec, from the debates on the Quebec Act, and from contemporary pamphlets that, in spite of some evidence to the contrary, the Quebec Act was dictated by the dangerous situation in the American colonies. The passage cited is the conclusion of a lengthy analysis of the Act and a refutation of the views of Coffin.

   ... it seems to us that the evidence justifies the well-known opinion of Francois-Xavier Garneau as well as the more recent judgment of an English-speaking historian of our country "The Quebec Act was drawn up with an eye not on Quebec but on Boston."

   We may say that this theory is much more consistent with the substance of our charter and with what may be called its inner logic. Set in the light of its true causes it appears more clear than it really is; an act of reparation and of justice, but above all a subtle measure of political advantage. For example the meaning of the strange and mysterious manipulation of political boundaries may be seen very clearly. . . .

   This historical explanation is fully in accord with our own past traditions. We knew how to recognize and to give thanks for the providential intervention which saved the continent from Anglo-Saxon domination in the crisis of 1774. There are moments in history when God seems visibly to demonstrate his sovereign power over the course of history and the destiny of nations (*peuples*). Undoubtedly divine providence, more active even than Taine's "eternal chemist" controls and orders all things. Providence holds all the threads of the human drama. There appear in the history of the world and of every nation (*peuple*) situations, decrees, and events, unexpected, astonishingly and entirely unaccountable either by the natural course of events, or by the rebellious and capricious will of man. . . . the substance of history shows visible traces of the hand of God as the marble reveals the hand of the sculptor.[49]

The abbé Groulx is an interesting illustration in Canadian history of that tendency which became so strong in the totalitarian countries in the 1930's, of requiring that national history be written in harmony with correct ideological principles. Groulx offers no argument at all beyond that of "inner logic" to prove the motives of the British in the passing of the Quebec Act. The only facts he adduces are that some concessions were made to the English, and especially that they retained the majority in the Legislative Council. The fact that the British made some concessions to the Canadians and refrained from making some others is apparently for him sufficient evidence, without further inquiry, not only that their motive was political and self-interested, but that it referred to a situation beyond the boundaries of the colony. His theory, as he indicates in the last paragraph cited, particularly pleases him, because it confirms his view of the overriding power of God shown in the care of his people. Groulx thus tacitly repudiates the principles of the modern historian that history is a secular study, that is, a study bounded by time, and that no matter what may be the religious or philosophic or political views of the particular historian he must be prepared to base his findings on evidence and to submit them to a rigorous logical examination. Groulx's frankness and honesty are disarming. He does not see history from the secular viewpoint. He regards it rather as a means of spiritual enlightenment.

i. W. P. M. Kennedy[50]

The period of the 1920's sees the beginning of serious work on this period of Canadian history by mature and scholarly historians, taking full advantage not only of the invaluable Shortt and Doughty collection, but also of manuscript sources and transcripts in the Public Archives of Canada, notably the various series of Colonial Office papers and the Dartmouth Papers.

W. P. M. Kennedy was Professor of History at the University of Toronto. He was one of several historians of the British Isles whose interest in imperial and constitutional questions resulted in valuable contributions to Canadian historiography. Kennedy seems to have been determined to do what he could to redeem Canadian history from the dullness of style which had settled over it like a blight. In this he succeeded. His style is spirited, even sparkling, and occasionally eloquent. This, and the fact that the essay on the Quebec Act is only one chapter of a major work on the Canadian constitution, help to explain a number of casual and even inaccurate references to some significant matters. For example, Kennedy states that "the whole body of French civil law was revived" (p. 51). Although he later quotes the exact words of the Act he does not appear to have noted that the "laws and customs of Canada" were not identical with the laws of France, or that the now famous and much debated phrase "property and civil rights" was apparently chosen with special care in order to exclude those parts of Canadian law (ecclesiastical law, for example) which were deemed inappropriate. He is insufficiently aware of the distinction between the Executive and Legislative Councils (p. 53). He refers to the Legislative Council as having the power to levy taxes, whereas the Act clearly gives it the power only to authorize the levy of taxes by local authorities (p. 54). He speaks of commercial matters as coming "under a French code"; yet, as the reports of the law officers (which he uses) would have told him, "code" was hardly the word to use of French or English law at the time. He states that the order to Carleton to communicate to his Council his instructions on all matters requiring their advice and consent is clear evidence that the government meant the instructions on English law to be carried out. But this order was a routine part of the Governor's instructions and therefore cannot be assumed to have had any special significance in relation to the policy of the Quebec Act.

Kennedy says, moreover, that "the saving clause guarding the King's ecclesiastical supremacy disappeared in the legalizing of the clerical rights and dues" (p. 57),[51] whereas, in fact it did not disappear, and its presence in the Act was a cause of considerable anxiety to the conscientious Bishop Briand whom Carleton endeavoured to relieve by telling him to take the oath and believe what he liked. He refers to "many" honourable and blameless officials in Quebec and to "many" others who were neither the one nor the other, without asking himself whether "many" is the right word for the mere handful of civil officers (good or bad) who were available to the administration at that time. In the same way he speaks of the "many forms" of the Quebec Bill before it was introduced into the House of Lords. Three drafts have been found, and the existence of at least one other may be deduced, but "many" must remain a guess. As to the reference to the old constitution before 1774—"a bone of contention, a legal stumbling block, a fly in the administrative ointment," these metaphors do not illuminate, they bewilder. Not one is exactly right, and the final one, suggesting an irritating imperfection only, is totally misleading. The patient would-be learner may pay too dearly for Kennedy's undoubtedly engaging style.

Kennedy has read carefully his only serious predecessor in this field, Victor Coffin. He has also read Adam Shortt's review of Coffin. He refers to Coffin as "useful, but narrow in outlook and lacking in wide historical background." On the important question of the motive behind the policy of the Quebec Act he agrees with Adam Shortt in attending almost exclusively to Carleton's despatches and attributing the policy to Carleton's influence with the ministry.

We know that the reports were practically pigeon-holed for years and were only considered in relation to practical politics late in 1773. We know that when the Act assumed its final form, almost every legal and expert opinion was rejected, and Carleton's ideas were almost completely incorporated. It is necessary to trace the causes behind these facts. Carleton undoubtedly, with Murray and Cramahé, was always well-disposed to the French-Canadians. He, with his brother governors and administrators, looked on their conquest as a mere accident in a wider and more complicated issue than colonial jealousies. Through no fault of their own they were treated as pawns on the chessboard of European diplomacy. Carleton, however, was a practical soldier, and he had no training in political thinking. There is no need to discount his soldierly and gentlemanly kindness to the conquered, in making a study of his relations to the problem of government which was forced upon him. He was too matter of fact in action to be misled wilfully by sentiment. All along he appears to have had definite opinions on the Canadian situation, which time and experience developed along their initial lines. As early as 1767 he had begun to relate Canada to the world, and to see the strategical position which the province would hold should the southern colonies prove recalcitrant. The defences of the country and the guarding of communications with New York assumed serious proportions in his mind, and already he heard thousands of troops march at the beginning of a colonial war. While Carleton had his mind fixed on what appeared to him the only vital issue as far as Quebec was concerned, he was informed that the Cabinet was seeking light on a new parliamentary constitution for the province, especially in connection with the blending of laws to satisfy all the inhabitants. His official report has been considered and was probably tied up in red tape with its fellows. His correspondence, however, was not overlooked. Here we find that official report amplified and explained. To a mind full of a military situation the Cabinet brought a political problem, and in all the dispatches that follow, that problem is seen through the eyes of a soldier, who anticipated a war in which he and the province over which he presided would play perhaps a decisive part.[52]

Kennedy then summarizes Carleton's despatches. He argues that they are specific evidence for the proposition which is, on the face of it, probable, that "it is impossible . . . to isolate the Quebec Act, unless the history of the North American continent from 1766 to 1774 is to be considered as consisting of watertight compartments" (p. 62). He mentions the fact that the King's message of March 7, 1774, to Parliament seemed to group the Quebec Act with the intolerable acts and he cites William Knox as supporting the contention that the Quebec Act was passed with the colonies in mind. And so, says Kennedy, "The purpose of the Act thus takes on another aspect than that of generosity and good will, largely though these undoubtedly figured in it":

> North and his advisors make it plain that the colonists were not quite undeceived in including it among the oppressive acts, and Knox discloses the whole spirit of the scheme. Canada was to be a military base, held quiet by an endowed church, a vast hinterland, a satisfied *noblesse,* a recognized priesthood, French civil law, and a disciplined and obedient population. The policy of Governor Carleton became the policy of the British Cabinet. We can now understand why Carleton hid his instructions during the crucial days in Canada. He intended that no concessions should be made to the British, for fear especially of offending the seigniors on whom his reliance was placed.[53]

Kennedy does not explicitly answer Coffin's arguments. It is interesting to notice that Coffin concentrates on the policy which appeared to be evolving in Britain between the years 1764 and 1770, whereas Kennedy, like others who agree with him, tends to emphasize the tenor of Carleton's despatches and the fact that whatever might have been suggested, nothing was done until the critical year, 1774. This does not necessarily mean that the Act was intended to provoke or to injure the other colonies, although Kennedy seems to assume that it does. His evidence does not really do more than show that Britain was concerned at the dangerous situation to the south, that the authorities were anxious to have a stable government in this alien and potentially dangerous colony to the north, and that for one reason or another they were not moved to action until the American crisis was upon them. Kennedy does not quite meet Coffin's contention that whatever the effect of the Act may have been, its purpose was to insure good and just government in Quebec and that its character was determined by the needs of the province itself and not by the situation in the colonies to the south.

Kennedy remarks that "in that subtle tantalizing world of human motive and human endeavour it is seldom possible to reconstruct history, had circumstances been different" (p. 70), yet he does consider, as McArthur does, the wisdom of the Quebec Act from the long-range viewpoint. Like McArthur he comes to somewhat ambiguous conclusions. He agrees with him in approving and in emphasizing the subsequent benefit of the religious clauses.

> The provisions granted in the Act to the Roman Catholic Church are remarkable, when the legal disabilities in England are recalled.
>
> It was a blessing for Canada that the Quebec Act settled the status of the Roman catholic church and removed it for generations out of that *damnosa haereditas*—religious politics. Had its position been left in the air without a statute behind it, the coming of the United Empire Loyalists might have added another war of religion to the tragedies of history. As it was, the transition to a new constitution was infinitely less complicated. It is fair to state, however, that in the width of the concessions and in the comprehensiveness of the guarantees, little place was left for give and take, and there was thus eliminated much of the sweet reasonableness of compromise.[54]

Kennedy also reflects McArthur in the rather uneasy balancing between a feeling of regret that French-Canadians were not assimilated and a piously orthodox tribute to their value in contemporary Canadian life.

> The Act laid on Quebec the old seigneurial and ecclesiastical system and buttressed up institutions which were already losing hold on the *habitants*. It is also claimed that the presence of a solid

French-Canadian group in modern Canada with all its attendant political difficulties can be traced to the folly of the Act. Many political thinkers, quite apart from racial and religious prejudices, believe that a less complete recognition of French-Canadianism in 1774 would have been acceptable to the French Canadians and would have eliminated such problems as are evident today in relation to race, creed and education . . .

. . . Quebec has brought essential and vital and characteristic gifts to the life of Canada, and they can be traced to the influence of the Roman catholic church satisfied in 1774. . . . One thing is certain, the Quebec Act strengthened the imperial tie, and we may too lightly exaggerate the defects and too lightly appreciate the virtues.[55]

These two passages have been brought together although separated by a page or two of text because they indicate the unease that many English-speaking historians experienced in dealing with an Act which they believed to be critical in the development of the country. Kennedy and McArthur as liberal nationalists would probably have agreed with Lord Durham that the building of a nation and the operation of parliamentary institutions are simpler in a homogeneous society. At the same time, they would not categorize the special character of Quebec as a regrettable thing and their honesty would compel them to recognize the many virtues of Quebec society. But Kennedy even more than McArthur, gives the impression that however great the virtues of French civilization may be, they are associated with strong political inconveniences. The rather vague conclusion to the discussion of the Quebec Act is typical of this attitude: "All that can be hoped for, in dealing with such a question as the Quebec Act, is to set down naught in malice, and to attempt to avoid the advocate in trying to be the judge."[56] What is interesting to the present day reader is that Kennedy, although he treats the matter as an open question, almost assumes that the Quebec Act was decisive in preserving the integrity of the French Canadians as a special group, an assumption that many if not most historians today would say is barely warranted by the evidence as we know it.

j. Reginald Coupland[57]

Reginald Coupland picks up and amplifies Kennedy's passing reference to the importance of the Quebec Act in maintaining and strengthening the imperial tie. He was a historian of the British Empire, deeply interested in the Act as an early expression of the policy of the Second British Empire, the policy of toleration and acceptance of the customs of peoples alien in language and religion, which was the foundation for the emerging concept of the Commonwealth of Nations. He wrote in the brief period of optimism which followed the First World War, when nineteenth century liberal nationalism appeared to be coming into its own. Coupland confined himself largely to printed sources. Of these he made full use. Unlike Kennedy, he, with Coffin, dismisses the idea of sinister motives in the Quebec Act. He develops a view, current among the Canadians themselves in the eighteenth century, that not only were the concessions to French Canadians justified on the grounds of humanity and the practical needs of government, but that Britain was in effect committed to them by the terms of the articles of capitulation and the peace treaty. In other words, mysterious motives explored by earlier writers may simply have been respect for public pledges. There is certainly much in contemporary comments to support this view; what made the problem so awkward for the government was that the promises made in the Proclamation were public pledges too. Coupland, however, follows Coffin and Kennedy in reading the Act precisely in the light of the instructions. Having discussed Article 12 (see above, p. 60), he adds:

Clearly these Instructions and the Draft Ordinance taken together went very far to meet the British claim. There is no vague promise now of future modifications of the French law when circumstances may require it. There is no talk now of a period of preparation for the jury-system. The Draft Ordinance provides at any rate optional juries at once; and it is the plain suggestion of the Instructions that Carleton and his Council should proceed to legislate for the application of English law, at least in part, to all civil actions other than those concerned with the ownership of land or the property of persons dying intestate—a drastic departure from the 'basis' of French law established by the Quebec Act. The difference between this policy and the language held by ministers in Parliament is unmistakable. Ultimate concessions to the British minority they had always contemplated; but now, because they were growing uneasy about British sentiment in the other colonies or because they were feeling the effect of pressure from the City or because Carleton had left England, they were bent on speeding up the process of concession.

Similarly as regards the statutory right of *habeas corpus* ministers were ready, it seems, in January to concede to the British minority what they had refused in June. They had sat silent then while Burke and Chatham scolded them for withholding from British subjects such as an essential element of British liberty; but now, behind the scenes, they spoke the language of the Opposition as if it had always been their own. [There follows a quotation of Article 13. See above, p. 60.][58]

Coupland in fact has discovered in the Quebec Act an admirable piece of legislation, right, he believes, in motive, and admirable in its results. He also does what no previous historian of the Quebec Act has done, in pointing out that any attempt at the extinction of the French Canadians would probably have been fruitless, so that the action of the British government, although he believes it to have been dictated by good motives, also represents the only practical solution to the problem.

. . . Did not the Quebec Act, like some ghastly injury of childhood, stunt and spoil the future life of Canada?

If the facts of that distant time have been truly stated in this essay, the first answer to such doubts and questions is evident. It is probable, in the highest degree, that, if the policy of the Quebec Act had not been adopted, Canada would have been lost to the British Empire in 1775, and no distinct Canadian nation could ever have come into being.

And the second answer is also clear. The contrary policy—the suppression of French-Canadian nationality—was in its essentials precluded by the terms of the Capitulations and the Treaty of Paris. The Roman Catholic religion and, in part at least, the French-Canadian civil law could not have been suppressed without a violation of public faith.

Apart, moreover, from the antecedent treaty-rights and apart from the subsequent dangers of the American invasion, it is difficult to believe that the policy of suppression was really practicable. The French-Canadians might have been deprived of their law, their Church of its legalized tithes, and their language of all official recognition. But would such measures, would even harsher measures, have succeeded in destroying French-Canadian nationality? There

are many examples in history, and some in very recent history, to
show how hard it is for one nation to fuse another nation's life into
its own, unless indeed the fusion be mutual and voluntary. For
nationality is at root a spiritual thing and difficult to kill. Nor was it
in New France in 1774 a young and tender growth: the French-
Canadians had been rooted there for a century and a half. Nor,
again, were they, like the French of Louisiana when it was annexed
to the United States, a small minority in a great English-speaking
state: the position was precisely the reverse. Under these circumstances, the French-Canadians might have been compelled to obey
the English law; but, once the spirit of national revolt had been
aroused, no power could have compelled them to speak the English
tongue. Nor could penal laws have forced the French-Canadians
any more than they could force the Irish, to abjure their faith; and
so long as their Church survived, the mainspring of their nationality
would have remained unbroken. Forcible fusion, in fact, must have
proved if it had ever been adopted, a futile policy.

A futile and—let it be frankly said—a vicious policy. Public
opinion in these days will not readily accept the doctrines of inevitable national antagonism, that nationality must fight or die,
must kill or be killed; that, if two nationalities exist within a single
state, 'one is the hammer and the other is the anvil'. To the modern
mind, indeed, it would seem a crime to have tried to stamp out
French nationality in Canada, a crime not only against the French-
Canadians but against all Canadians of all time. For it cannot be
questioned that, whatever the transient drawbacks and difficulties
may be, Canada is the richer for its twofold national heritage, for
being peopled from a Celtic as well as an Anglo-Saxon stock, for
its pride in French as well as British customs and traditions, for its
use of the two greatest languages and its access to the two greatest
literatures of the modern world. A multi-national state, moreover,
is not merely richer, in its complexity and variety, than a uni-
national state: it is, as Acton argued long ago, a higher species of
political organism, a greater achievement in civilized life, provided
that its component nationalities are at once free and united.

Nor, lastly, can it be admitted that freedom in Canada is a permanent obstacle to unity. These are still early days in the life of the
Dominion, and such a final judgement . . . is almost absurdly premature. Already, indeed, . . . the prospect has grown fairer; there
is a better understanding, a closer concord in the recognition of a

common patriotism, between French and British-Canadians today than there has ever been since 1837; and only the blackest pessimists can refuse to believe that, in due course of time, Canada will grow into a unity as real and lasting as the unity of Britain. When that day comes, the last doubt as to the statesmanship of the authors of the Quebec Act will have faded away. No one will claim, then or now, that Carleton and North and the rest were gifted with super-human foresight or inspired by the ideals of a later age. They were only concerned to meet the needs of their own day: they were simply trying to honour their treaty-pledges and to conciliate a conquered people. Practical men, they achieved those practical ends; but their achievement was greater and more lasting than they knew. For they had acted in accordance with political principles of permanent force and universal application—that, in the long run, the unity of the whole is all the stronger for the diversity of its parts, and that on fidelity to the old, deep loyalties of local or provincial or national life, and only indeed on that sure foundation, can be built, if men are wise and patient, a broader and more general communion of human fellowship and service.[59]

k. Chester Martin[60]

Chester Martin, a Canadian and a firm supporter of the Common-wealth idea, offers the liberal counter argument against Coupland's defence of the Quebec Act as a recognition of the rights of conquered peoples. He condemned the policy as illiberal, the motives as hostile to the American colonies, and the results, as the cause of the destruction of the first Empire and enduring hostility between French- and English-Canadians. In opposition to most legal authorities, then and since, he believed that the plan of 1769 (see above, p. 24) could have been implemented without parliamentary legislation. He blamed the Quebec Act as an unfortunate substitute for the 1769 plan, dictated by Carleton and accepted by those who were increasingly committed to co-ercion in America.

Martin, like Kennedy and Shortt, is inclined to attach importance to Carleton's letters as giving the active motive for the Quebec Act. He suggests that the Act was dictated by the desire to avoid the "catas-trophe shocking to think of," that it failed in its purpose and not only failed to prevent but possibly played its part in provoking the disaster of the American Revolution.

Thus the *Quebec Act,* which is now chiefly remarkable for its
subsequent influence upon Canadian history and politics, belonged
in its origin and in its context essentially to the age before the
deluge. It was devised to preclude a 'Catastrophe shocking to think
of'. Beyond all question, for weal or for woe, it was not without
influence both upon the beginnings and upon the subsequent course
of the American Revolution: though scarcely perhaps in the way its
advocates intended. Chatham and Burke and Fox thus viewed the
Quebec Act in a background then for the last time contemplated
with hope by British statesmen—the background of an undivided
Empire. Let it be conceded that this, the greatest issue of that generation or of any other, had the first claim upon the thought and
allegiance of public men. And indeed the *Quebec Bill* was attacked
not because it ignored the American situation but because, as the
opponents of the Bill came to believe, it dealt with the American
situation upon principles so reactionary that none thereafter could
mistake their import.[61]

Far from rejoicing in the religious provisions of the Quebec Act
as precluding religious strife, Martin sees the Quebec Act as inter-
posing a barrier between the French Canadians and the Loyalists who
were destined to come into the province in a few years. Britain, in
making necessary provisions for the Loyalists, was then forced to act
in apparent bad faith toward the Canadians and so the concession,
for example, of an assembly which earlier would have been a healing
and uniting influence, was looked upon as an impostion.

. . . and when one compares the comprehensive project of the
Board of Trade in 1769 with that which supplanted it in 1774, the
difference in time, in spirit, and in principle, becomes in truth unmistakable. Had French-Canadians, who have shown themselves
perhaps the most politically minded people in Canada, been introduced into full British citizenship in 1769 in the spirit of magnani-
mous toleration, might not such a union at such a time have enriched
Canadian history and Canadian politics for all generations to come?
After the *mariage de convenance* in 1774 upon the basis of arbitrary governance, even the loyalist migrations—the forgotten step-
children of the union—could be regarded by Church and seigneur
as a violation of the spirit of the *Quebec Act.* And when these step
children proceeded to vindicate their right to the patrimony, can it

be a matter of surprise that the step-mother began to reflect ruefully upon the inducements which the other contracting party had employed in 1774? Let it be remembered that whatever had been the attitude of the *habitants* who had not been consulted, the Church and seigneurs, as a whole, had resolutely 'played the game'. And thus representative institutions after 1791 were from the first but step-children in Lower Canada. In such a household, charges of self-interest and bad faith soon poisoned domestic relations; and when the other branch of the family in Upper Canada was brought in at the Union to readjust the balance, it is not difficult to understand the resentment of French Canada. Bitter and uncharitable though many of the judgments of Girouard and of LaFontaine may have been, who can deny that they had reason for their reflections, and that a nobler conception of the destiny of the two races under British institutions at the outset might have gone far to establish the golden rule of toleration and of compromise?[62]

Martin forgets, however, that LaFontaine resented the arbitrary treatment of the Canadians and the threat to their language, and that he, with Bedard and Parent, as well as with their predecessors *Les Vrais Patriotes* (see above, p. 28), looked on the assembly rather than on the Quebec Act as the source of their rights. The seigneurial party had, it is true, been reactionary, but the Quebec Act certainly had not unfitted French Canadians for appreciating and using an assembly. Martin ventures into the risky area of what might have been, and does not produce any convincing evidence.

I. A. L. Burt[63]

A. L. Burt made by far the most thorough study yet undertaken of the primary sources available for the whole period. He embodied his findings in a solid, authoritative but eminently readable volume. Although he was mindful of the new emphasis on economic and social history, his interests were primarily political. In keeping also with the temper of the period in which he wrote, he paid relatively little attention to religious history. He follows his immediate predecessors in looking at the Act most carefully in connection with the instructions. In general he agrees with Coupland and approves the Act as generous and statesmanlike, accepting gracefully the inevitable "French fact."

Burt, like Coffin, repudiates the idea of an ulterior motive in the Quebec Act. He supports his position in detail, carefully answering all the arguments advanced to show that, as was said in the debates on the Act, there was "something that squints and looks dangerous to the inhabitants of the other colonies."

He discusses the suggestion that the timing of the Act is suspicious. Had it been intended to deal with the situation in Quebec without prejudice to any other colony, why, it has been asked, was it not passed much earlier? Burt does not mention Fowler Walker's doubts about the validity of the existing government, doubts which according to Walker could only be removed by parliamentary legislation. He does, however, show that the government was not entirely convinced of the truth of Walker's statement. He quotes the Colonial Secretary Hillsborough to show that even as late as December 1771 the government still hoped to avoid the publicity of legislation.

> In December, 1771, the secretary of state lamented the delay but affirmed that it was unavoidable because the problem was one of such "delicacy and importance" and "almost every department of government" had to be consulted. Very probably the rising tide of troubles in the old colonies was also responsible. He now admitted the possibility of further delay, for he said, "I am not without apprehension that it may at last be found necessary that the opinion of the king's servants should be submitted to parliament before any final settlement can take place." Obviously the way was dark.[64]

After a consideration of the various reports presented to the ministry and a statement of the passing of the Quebec Act (and also of the passing of the four penal acts), Burt continues:

> The old colonies naturally leaped to the conclusion that the Quebec Act was a blow aimed through Canada at them. By extending Canada's boundaries down the Ohio, did it not threaten to coop them up on the narrow Atlantic seaboard? Did it not establish Roman Catholicism, the very antithesis of their religious faith? Did it not deny a popular government, the very article of their political faith? What could be the meaning of all this unless it was intended to arm Canada to crush their economic, religious, and political liberties? Indeed, Britain seemed to have stepped into France's shoes in America, and the old menace, which they had thought forever banished in 1760, loomed up darker than ever.

The conclusions drawn by the Americans at the time have been since supported by an appeal to the way in which the measure was passed. The government rushed it through parliament at the fag end of the session and withheld all the official papers which had been connected with its preparation. The opposition called for the reports of the governor and of the law officers, but their motions were rejected by a two to one vote . . .

Against these arguments of the Americans then and of others later there is a good deal to be said . . . The main character of the act was mostly determined before people in England heard of the tea party that suddenly brought on the American crisis. The new boundary line, foreshadowed in a letter which Dartmouth wrote Cramahé on December 1, 1773, had long been an obvious necessity. An assembly seems to have been out of the question from the beginning of 1771, and any doubts lingering in Maseres' mind were removed by a statement which he received from Lord North in the summer of 1773. The feudal system was restored to its full vigor in 1771 as an earnest of legal concessions repeatedly promised. . . .

The way in which the bill was railroaded through parliament is no proof of any evil motive on the part of its sponsors. It simply proves beyond all shadow of doubt that the coming of the Revolution merely precipitated the birth of the Quebec Act. The foundations of the British Empire in America were shaking. Canada might be swallowed up in an earthquake unless her constitution were immediately established on a firm basis.[65]

Burt repeats, although he does not acknowledge, Victor Coffin's argument that if the Quebec Act had been "penal" the fact need not have been concealed.

There is no justification for saying that [the majority] voted under orders. The opposition's taunts that the government had some concealed purpose in framing the bill need not be taken seriously. Parliament had eagerly passed four penal statutes against the old colonies, and if the government designed this as a fifth, its supporters could have advanced no stronger argument for hurrying it through the house.[66]

On the denial of an assembly Burt deals directly and specifically with Chester Martin, with whose work and opinions he was of course familiar.

It has been maintained that the British government committed a fatal blunder in abandoning the plan of 1769. But should it be blamed for acting on the advice of the governor, the chief justice, and the attorney-general, who, much as they differed on other points, were unanimously against the board of trade's proposal of representative government? . . . Canada in 1774 was not Nova Scotia in 1758. . . . The Acadians were ignored when an assembly was called in Halifax, but the Canadians could not be ignored. Had an assembly been created without them, as the English-speaking minority really wanted, their hearts would most probably have turned back to France. On the other hand, had these newly-conquered people been admitted to an assembly, the risk would have been tremendous. Under any circumstances such an experiment would have been very bold, and the circumstances of the time were far from being auspicious.[67]

Burt, like Coupland, argues that any hardship in connection with the introduction of Canadian civil law would have been eliminated had Carleton attended to his instructions.

Had the instructions been carried out, the settlement of the laws would have worked no hardship upon the English-speaking minority. They suffered grievously because the instructions remained a dead letter. For this tragedy Carleton was to blame . . . he was the author of much of the iniquity which has been erroneously ascribed to the Quebec Act and to the government that passed it.[68]

Burt concludes by agreeing with Coupland that the Act was inevitable and, he believes, good.

French Canadians have praised the Quebec Act as the charter of liberties which saved their race in its time of trial; others who deplore the existence of French-Canadian self-consciousness have denounced the act for having made a real national unity impossible in Canada. Both exaggerate. Just as the chief value of the Magna Carta was posthumous—a rallying cry for later generations—so perhaps the greatest effect of the Quebec Act has been psychological. It is idle to imagine that the French of Canada could have been assimilated. Races have been merged in others, but only when the assimilated did not possess an old and fixed civilization, or when they were in a minority. Neither of these fundamental conditions existed in the colony. The French possessed a civilization as ancient and as fixed as that of the English, and they vastly outnumbered them. Not until the middle of the nineteenth century were there as many English as French in Canada. If the policy of 1763 had been developed and enforced, instead of being abandoned, it might have driven Canada out of the British Empire and into the American Union. For all its denial of an assembly, the Quebec Act embodied a new sovereign principle to the British Empire: the liberty of non-English-speaking peoples to be themselves.[69]

In this important passage Burt shows more clearly and definitively than any previous writer has done that Durham's dream of an easy assimilation was only a dream. The argument has been found convincing and few people today would question its validity.

Two statements in this passage, however, may be questioned. It is not certain that French Canadians have valued the Quebec Act as a charter of liberties as much as some English-Canadian historians appear to think. An examination of the issues of *Le Canadien* from its beginning until the Rebellion of 1837 does not show any particular preoccupation with the Quebec Act. That investigation, along with the work of Jacques Monet (see below, p. 133, note 8), suggests that the notion of the Quebec Act as an unalterable charter may have been largely confined to the seigneurial party and that it was brushed aside by the new middle class radicals who got control of the Assembly within a decade of its being established in 1791. This question is probably worth further investigation.

The statement that the Quebec Act embodied a new sovereign principle of the British Empire, the liberty of non-English peoples to be themselves, although attractive to historians concerned with the Commonwealth idea, must also be modified in the light of the instructions to the Governor in relation to the liberties granted to the Church of Rome in the province. These instructions are detailed by Burt, who comments only that they were ignored until a generation later when an attempt to enforce them helped to precipitate racial strife. This statement is entirely correct and, if one is to consider the Quebec Act as it was enforced, the religious instructions are of no importance. Burt, however, does not consider the Quebec Act as it was enforced. He defends it specifically by insisting on reading with the Act the instructions on the changes and reforms desirable in the civil law. There seems, however, to be no reason for including in the policy of the Act certain of the instructions and omitting others, and if the religious instructions are considered a part of the integral policy of the Act it can hardly be considered as granting to non-English peoples the liberty to be themselves. The Church was the most characteristic and influential institution of the Canadians and any policy hostile to the continuation of the Church must certainly be considered as hostile to the Canadian community as it existed in the 1760's.

3. ECONOMIC HISTORIANS

While political historians in the 1920's were using material recently made available by new and authoritative studies on the constitutional and political aspects of the Quebec Act, others had been looking at the colony not as an illustration of principles of law, liberty and the rights of nations, but as a place where men continued to do as they had always done—seek their fortune in the fur trade. They noted that the fur trader and the land seeker have certain permanent characteristics unaffected by their political allegiance. The work of these historians has given a whole new perspective to the post-conquest period and has thrown new light on the policy of the Quebec Act and in particular on the debatable boundary clause, that part of the Act most offensive to the American colonies.

a. C. W. Alvord[70]

C. W. Alvord is as much a political as an economic historian, but it was his work that directed attention to the economic aspects of the Quebec Act. As the title of his work shows, he made a detailed study of the development of British policy in the old Northwest. He showed how Britain's unsuccessful attempts at looking after her own imperial interests and at the same time mediating between the rights of the Indian peoples and the demands, not only of settlers but of land speculators, were a major cause of the American Revolution, and ultimately the occasion of the boundary clause of the Quebec Act.

Alvord discusses the various attempts of successive ministries in that very unstable political era to implement the general policy of the Proclamation of 1763, the creation of a temporary reserve patrolled by a military force, open to licensed fur traders but closed for the time to present settlers and to land speculators. He shows that, apart from the delay caused by unstable ministries and want of complete agreement in Britain, the policy was doomed to failure by American opposition and American refusal to contribute to the expense, a refusal which precipitated the disastrous taxation controversy. Alvord contends that, other plans having failed, the boundary clause of the Quebec Act was Britain's last attempt at solving the difficult frontier problem. The purpose was threefold: (a) to check the encroachments of settlers on Indian lands; (b) to provide government for the Canadian villages in the Illinois country; (c) to regulate the fur trade.

The main purpose of the Quebec Bill was the alleviation of the wrongs of the alien population of the North; but it was at the same time the vehicle for the promulgation of a new western policy. The extension of the boundaries of the province of Quebec so as to include the Old North West was the last effort of the mother country to throw the protection of the imperial power over at least a part of the Mississippi Valley in order to prevent the disorders of the region.

To the ministers these disorders always appeared very real, for the most unfavourable descriptions of frontier society were being constantly sent to the government by both colonial and English writers. From the beginning of their administration of Indian Affairs Sir William Johnson and John Stuart had reported to their superiors that the fur traders were sprung from the lowest classes, were men of unscrupulous character, and were accustomed to practice the lowest and meanest tricks on the Indians . . .

. . . [A second purpose was to provide civil government for the French settlements.] An inspired defender of the Quebec Act wrote, after describing the ills suffered by the French in these distant villages: "In this situation and in these circumstances what better can be done than to annex this country to Quebec, and subject the whole to the jurisdiction of that colony, to which the only lawful settlers in it were originally subject, and whose language, manners, inclination and religion are the same—. . ."

A third weighty reason for the extension of the boundary was the regulation of the fur trade. The failure of the colonies to agree upon some form of general administration of the Indian trade had resulted in the development of intolerable conditions in the region west of the mountains. Both Lord Hillsborough and Lord Dartmouth, after studying the problem, had reached the conclusion that the only method of correcting the existing evils was by an Act of Parliament. The Quebec Bill offered the means. The Old Northwest provided the finest furs in abundance. By placing this territory under such a government as was provided for Quebec the necessary regulations could be made.[71]

For the rest, Alvord shows in detail that, although the Quebec Act coincided in time with the penal acts, it represented for Quebec a policy which had been maturing since 1764, and that every one of its main provisions had been agreed on before the news of the Boston Tea Riot reached London. Alvord supports and amplifies Coffin's case, to which he refers, and he precedes Burt in his careful examination of evidence on the preparation of the Act. It is difficult to understand how Chester Martin, with the works of Coffin and Alvord at his disposal, could so easily have taken up once more the old penal theory of the Quebec Act.

Of particular interest in Alvord's work is his contention that throughout this period the problems of the Mississippi Valley were foremost in the minds of British statesmen concerned with North America. He suggests indeed that the great problem in Quebec caused by the apparent introduction of English law was a result of a mistake on the part of the authorities in issuing the Proclamation of 1763. He has found some slight evidence to suggest that a special treatment for Quebec was intended and that only as a result of haste in the issuing of the Proclamation immediately after a change in government was Quebec included with the other colonies and opened to English settlers with a promise of English law.

This theory is now generally discarded as being based on very slight evidence. It is interesting, however, to find the germ of it in the report on the laws of Quebec by Advocate General James Marriott, who says ". . . so it should seem as if this proclamation had been copied inadvertently, and in the hurry of office, from some former proclamation relative to Nova Scotia, or some other *unsettled* British colony, inviting persons to emigrate thither from their mother-country; and that the reflection never entered the thoughts of the drawers up of this proclamation, that Canada was a conquered province, full of inhabitants, and already in possession of a legal establishment."[72]

b. Marjorie G. Reid[73]

While historians in Canada still tended to concentrate on politics, constitutional autonomy, and French-English relations, the new emphasis on economic history could hardly fail to direct their attention to the very obvious fact that in a fur-trading colony seized by one great commercial empire from another, admittedly with an eye to commercial profit as well as to strategic advantage, economic considerations were likely to have their influence on legislation. Even though in Burt's work political considerations were still central, the economic interpretation of Canadian history had already begun and was to be of increasing importance throughout the next decade.

In 1925 Marjorie Reid undertook to investigate the problems of fur traders in the Ohio country and the northwest after 1763. She examined not only the well-known C. O. 42 series in the Public Archives but other Colonial Office series dealing more particularly with matters of trade. She does not, like Alvord, go into the political history of Great Britain, but, confiining herself to North America, she is satisfied with showing that whatever other motives may have existed for the boundary clause it can be quite sufficiently explained and defended by the problems of the western administration and of the fur trade. She is, of course, indebted to Alvord for opening up the problem. Her article is of special interest in that it emphasizes both the advantages of Quebec in relation to the fur trade and the initiative of the Canadian fur traders. Her thesis is that there is no need to look farther than the situation and the interests of the St. Lawrence colony to find the reason for the extension of the boundary which was dictated, she suggests, by geography and history rather than by contemporary politics.

The Quebec Act of 1774 re-annexed to Quebec the north-west, from the Ohio on the south to the Mississippi on the west. The extraordinary gap in the documentary sources between 1771 and 1774 makes it impossible to trace all the reasons for this decision of the ministers. It is, however, clear that the territorial provisions of the Quebec Act did not, like the "intolerable acts" of 1774, represent a sudden decision to restrain and punish the offending colonists. They were, as Lord North claimed during the parliamentary debate upon the Act, the logical result of several years' experiment in the administration of the western hinterland. If the whole west had been British, its problems might have been solved gradually. Commercial expansion might have led industrial enterprise from one locality to another, and profits might have kept pace with expenditure. The presence of the French on the Mississippi called for a strong well-governed colony in the Illinois. So Shelburne had thought in 1768, but the fatal necessity for domestic economy in Britain and the want of an adequate system of American revenue killed the enterprise. The colonial secretaries who succeeded Shelburne lacked the courage to face the question of governing the Illinois. The course of local events was, however, forcing another solution. The first step was that the Canadian merchants secured, for themselves, and for all the British traders, the privilege of dealing directly with the Indian tribes. Since they possessed in the Great Lakes the best route for trade, and since they had acquired a commercial machine better adapted to the circumstances of the west, the Quebec merchants outdid the Ohio merchants. It seemed as if Quebec must inevitably control the fur trade. After Shelburne's plan of barrier colonies had been rejected, and when the disaffection of the Atlantic colonists made necessary an immediate settlement of the west, the obvious course of action was to annex it to Quebec. The continued presence of the French on the continent and the enterprise of Canadian merchants had dragged Canada into a prominence over the other British colonies which the circumstances of the eighty thousand French settlers hardly warranted. The fundamental cause was geographical. Quebec was the chief ocean port of the Great Lakes system, and New Orleans was the ocean port of the Mississippi. A century earlier LaSalle had realized the significance of the two routes when he opened the Mississippi to trade. Geography and history together were stronger at first than the ambitions of the American colonists, and therefore the French colony on the St. Lawrence played for a time the leading role in the drama of western development.[74]

Marjorie Reid's reference to "the extraordinary gap in the documentary sources between 1771 and 1774" refers to one of the arguments brought forward by those who thought they detected a concealed and sinister motive for the Quebec Act. They found that discussion of general policy in the Colonial Office correspondence apparently died away after 1770. Occasional references even suggest a suspicion that material might have been deliberately destroyed. The gap, however, is easy to explain. Carleton, the chief source of information to the ministry, was in England from 1770 until the passing of the Act. His temporary successor Cramahé, was not in the confidence of the ministry. As all the people with special knowledge were in London, much of the business was presumably done by conversation and by the fragmentary notes and memoranda which do survive in the Dartmouth Papers. The situation is frustrating to the historian but was no doubt as convenient to those concerned as telephone conversations are today.

c. Louise Kellogg[75]

Louise Kellogg, an American scholar, should not perhaps be classed among economic historians as the purpose of her article is rather to examine the political, strategic, and what one might call the humane motives of the boundary clause. Her concentration on this aspect of the Quebec Act, however, makes it convenient to group her with historians whose primary interest is economic. She draws attention to a fact not much discussed by historians but familiar to any who read the correspondence of the day, that the deportation of the Acadian exiles was not regarded by everyone as in itself an outrage against humanity. James Murray, who was a conspicuously humane governor writing during the military regime, refers to the possibility (which had clearly been mentioned to him) that the Canadians living in the upper country might be deported as a result of the prohibition of settlement in the Ohio country. Miss Kellogg shows that Hillsborough and Gage revived what had apparently been an earlier scheme in 1772 and considered the wholesale deportation of French-speaking inhabitants of Vincennes, as well as those from the area of Michilmackinac who were now left without regular civil government.

This was the position of affairs in the first months of 1772. Hillsborough, who had been studying the situation during the four years of his tenure as secretary of state, had concluded to remove the garrisons of Fort de Chartres and its supply post, Fort Pitt. The French inhabitants were to be deported, beginning with the smaller settlements like that of Vincennes, and any, such as those near Detroit and Mackinac, that could prove no legal title to their lands. Detroit was to be maintained for the present, as many English were flocking thither. The Illinois settlers were to be induced or cajoled, or forced into removing to some other colony. The commander-in-chief in America agreed with the secretary of state in England. In his famous phrase "Let the savages enjoy their Desarts in quiet"—lurked the germ of his plan to deport the French inhabitants and to keep the west permanently for an Indian reservation.

The fall of Hillsborough from power in August, 1772, saved the western French from a fate similar to that of the Acadian exiles. Lord Dartmouth who accepted the secretaryship was a humane man, whose mind could picture the fear and terror of these "new subjects of his Majesty" at the proposed removal. Dartmouth at once began to make inquiries and to change the policy with regard to the west. The small garrison left temporarily at Kaskaskia he ordered to be retained. He asked why civil government had not been granted to the Illinois inhabitants in response to their petition. "Under the Treaty of Paris the people of Illinois have a right to remain and should have protection." If their proposals for civil government were too absurd and extravagant, they should have some form of government that would be acceptable ...

What that form of government ought to be Dartmouth pondered long and earnestly. He wrote to Cramahé, then administrator of Canada, that there was no longer any hope of perfecting the policy with regard to the interior country which was contemplated when the Proclamation of 1763 was issued. It was not until the third draft of the Quebec Act that Dartmouth came forward with his proposal to extend the boundaries of Quebec to include all the western French settlements in that province ...

The great extent of country bounded by the Ohio River, the Great Lakes, and the Mississippi, in which are now five of the most flourishing states of the American Union, was, for the sake of its French inhabitants joined to Canada and taken from the American colonies, which claimed the rights of settlement therein. As is well known this was one of the grievances cited by the Americans in their Declaration of Independence. To avoid making exiles of the western French, the British ministers annexed this great region to their new Province of Quebec. The western French were well aware of the fate from which Dartmouth had saved them. Even when the Americans, under George Rogers Clark entered the Illinois four years later, the fear of deportation had not left them. "The French of that place [Kaskaskia]", he wrote, "expected to be deported, but begged that families should not be separated." The fate of the Acadians, so narrowly averted from their own lives, made them fearful even of the American who came as a liberator.[76]

d. D. G. Creighton[77]

It was Harold Adam Innis who was more than any other person responsible for turning Canadian historians to the study of the economic aspects of their history. Innis joined the staff of the University of Toronto in 1920 and became head of the Department of Political Economy in 1937. He presented as his doctoral thesis a history of the Canadian Pacific Railway. As a result of this study Innis began to see communications as the neglected key to Canadian history. This led him back to the early history of the country and to the fur trade. In 1930 he published *The Fur Trade in Canada*. Like Parkman before him, Innis insisted on seeing at first hand and in something of the old manner the country that he was to write about. His work has rightly been termed a landmark in Canadian history. Hitherto orthodox Canadian historians, nourished on the liberal nationalist and free-trade principles of nineteenth century Britain, had assumed that Canada had somehow grown in defiance of geography, cutting across the prevailing North-South lines of communication in North America. Innis explicitly countered this assumption by pointing out that the Dominion of Canada was a completely natural historic-geographic phenomenon. It represented, as he showed, the old empire of the fur trader, except for those large fragments, Ohio country and the Oregon territory, which had been lost by the fur trader to the encroaching American settler.

Donald Creighton, colleague and friend and ultimately the biographer of Innis, followed his highly suggestive but sometimes fragmentary study with the eloquent and persuasive *Commercial Empire of the St. Lawrence*, the first of a series of works by Creighton which cover almost every period of post-Conquest Canadian history. It represents a serious beginning of an important work of revision, the justification of Canada's existence in terms of geography and economics, and incidentally a new view of those two contentious Canadian characters, John A. Macdonald and the Canadian Pacific Railway.

Creighton's work deals with the Quebec Act from the viewpoint of the merchants whom Murray called "licentious fanaticks" and whom Creighton sees as daring men who, along with Canadians of French descent "would fight to realize the commercial empire of the St. Lawrence" (p. 21), against its rivals on the Bay and the Hudson River. Creighton sees the extension of the boundary by the Quebec Act as a recognition of "the facts of geography, the Western commercial supremacy of Canada, and the existence of Canadian settlements like Detroit," although he recognizes that there may have been other considerations. The rest of the Act he sees as at best anachronistic and, in the narrow interpretation given by Carleton and Haldimand, as a serious injury to the trading community.

The Quebec Act, which was a revival of the old feudal and absolutist structure of New France, coincided with the renewal of the old armed conflict between the northern colony and the Atlantic seaboard. The war seemed to justify the maintenance of the act unchanged; and a reactionary constitution became even more reactionary than its framers in England intended. For though the Quebec Act was designed to satisfy the supposed leaders of the French-Canadian majority in Quebec, it was not intended that the act should be applied, without modification, to the prejudice of the minority of

British-Canadian merchants. Carleton's new instructions contained
a number of moderate glosses upon the medieval austerity of the new
constitution. The legislature, which was supposed to interpret the
law of the act in the spirit of the instructions, was advised, in particular, to follow the British model of habeas corpus and "to consider
well" whether English laws might not be established in whole or in
part for all personal actions grounded upon debts, promises, contracts or agreements, whether of a mercantile or other nature. Unfortunately, while the medieval elements of the new constitution
were established by law, its modernities were merely suggested to a
council composed of soldiers, bureaucrats and landowners, instinc-
tively opposed to merchants and to middle-class reformers.

The result was certain. Carleton violated some of his instructions
and interpreted others in the spirit of his intense convictions; and
the perversion of the constitution was continued by the stolidly conservative Haldimand to the end of the war. Carleton created the
"Privy Council"—a body warranted only by a badly worded clause
in the instructions—and in this small, selected group was vested the
real political power in the colony. In January of 1777, the legislative
council met at last for its first effective session. The French-Canadian councillors had already shown themselves singularly indisposed
to repay the munificence of the British ministers in England by a
little generosity to the British merchants in Canada. Carleton failed
to communicate the clauses of his instructions which advised reform
in favour of the merchants, though by another clause of the same
instructions he was ordered to do so; and through Captain Cramahé,
his fellow-officer and his lieutenant-governor, he intimated that he
was entirely opposed to juries in civil suits. The council did not even
consider habeas corpus. It voted down optional juries and English
law in commercial suits; and it thus left the laws of New France
completely unaltered for the whole civil business of the Canadian
courts.[78]

Creighton goes on to show that, as A. L. Burt had suggested, English and French commercial laws were both based on the law merchant
of Europe. He states, however, that as the Council did not introduce
English commercial law and as the French *code marchand* had not
been regularly introduced into New France before the conquest, Canadian merchants could not use the general commercial law in either of
these national derivative forms, and the Canadian customs that were
undeniably applicable were unsuited to their problems.[79] Creighton is

the first writer who, ignoring the much-developed Durham thesis of the desirability of assimilating the Canadians, devotes himself to giving a case for the merchant group and to showing the immense importance of that group in the economic development of the country and even of the continent. Working on a narrow front he gives an effective and substantially sound case. It is not his purpose to deal in any detail with the Quebec Act; the main part of his work is concerned with the great expansion of the fur trade that occurred from the close of the American Revolution to the union of the companies in 1821.

The reader may be inclined to question the appropriateness of the repeated use of the word "medieval" without definition, almost as a term of abuse. There is plenty of evidence that the French system of land-holding had been adapted to the needs of the Canadian colony and, up to this time, had served them well enough. It was presumably no more medieval in its character than the traditional systems of land-holding practiced at that time in England and Scotland. Moreover, in using the word "munificence" to describe the concessions of the Quebec Act to French Canadians, Creighton is assuming without argument that Coupland's contention that most of the concessions of the Quebec Act were implicit in the capitulations is groundless. Creighton's simple, uncomplicated economic approach, which forces the reader to consider the well-being of what had always been a commercial colony from the commercial viewpoint, offers a very useful revision of the complex political-constitutional-social approaches. The illumination, however, although brilliant, is limited, and the implied condemnation of the Act as a whole can leave a false impression.

e. Fernand Ouellet[80]

Fernand Ouellet, like Creighton, concentrates on economic developments. His purpose, however, is to write a social as well as an economic history. An exponent of quantitative methods, he tends to see social and even political developments almost exclusively in terms of economic circumstances. He is more ambitious than Creighton, then, in that he appears to assume that economic factors are a sufficient explanation for social and political events (Creighton leaves more scope for human folly and wickedness).

Believing that racial and national antipathy between English and Canadians has been exaggerated as a political factor, Ouellet goes far to eliminate it altogether. One of the most important consequences of the conquest, he says, was the divorce between "the landed aristocracy which thought in terms of absolutism, feudalism and bureaucracy, and the bourgeoisie striving to redefine society in terms of its own values" (p. 96). In this context Ouellet sees the military and official class siding with the landed aristocracy against the minority mercantile group, English and Canadian.

The importance of the wishes and opinions of the first governors under the British regime over the Colonial Office has been greatly exaggerated. If our historians are to be believed, the French Canadians, frustrated by the vexing political situation in 1763, found in Murray and Carleton heroes apparently sent by Providence. This interpretation, because it does not take into consideration the general situation in the province at the time gives an epic quality to the story. But can it be believed that the program of 1763 would have been abandoned so quickly if economic growth had been rapid, if a massive immigration had developed in the province and if there had not been an American danger? Between 1763 and 1768 the total evolution of Quebec took such a form that the original policy appeared incomprehensible even to those who had defined it. In 1768 Hillsborough attributed "this original and fatal mistake" to misinterpretation, to ignorance and to the anarchy of the times. It was because the evolution of the colony appeared so different from the optimistic forecasts of earlier years that the English statesmen did not hesitate once the situation of which we have spoken was understood, to qualify their measures as a crime against humanity "a sort of severity if I remember right" wrote Carleton "never before practiced by any conqueror, even where the people, without capitulation, submitted to his will and discretion". This attitude of self-accusation at a moment when liberal ideas were gaining ground in England, indicates that at that date those in control in Canada and in England clearly understood the real tendencies of evolution in the colony. It remains true, however, that the presence of Murray and Carleton in the colony helped the British ministers to see clearly into the Canadian problem. Without them the change would have come more slowly. But even they could not have changed the policy of 1763 had not the expected immigration failed to take place.[81]

No doubt previous writers, preoccupied with the bulk of legal and constitutional material, have neglected the economic situation for which the evidence is more difficult to secure and possibly to interpret.

Ouellet's new approach, like Creighton's, is startling and illuminating. And yet both may be misleading if considered as adequate explanations and interpretations of the Quebec Act. Creighton ignores the political and legal origins of the Quebec Act. Ouellet offers a generalization which ignores not only the work of previous scholars, but the evidence of obviously relevant facts.

The extent of Murray's influence is difficult to determine. Perhaps his letters had some influence on the government before he was recalled in something like disgrace at the request of the merchants. After his exoneration he may perhaps have given advice and information, although the evidence is wanting. It is possible that the influence of Carleton has been somewhat exaggerated. This is the suggestion of V. T. Harlow (see below, p. 126), but for want of correspondence about the Act at the critical time, the evidence is inadequate for any definite statement. Certainly the belief that, failing a massive immigration, more attention should be paid to the needs of Canadians than to those of the English merchants was frequently expressed. But the most striking expression to this effect comes from Carleton himself: "Barring a catastrophe shocking to think of, this country must, to the end of time be peopled by the Canadian race . . ."[82] Ouellet assumes that the complete reversal, as it seems to him, of the policy of the Proclamation[83] comes only after 1768 when ministers were led to adopt it by unexpected economic developments. But this is to ignore Lord Mansfield's immediate and almost passionate protest[84] (December 24, 1764), the opinion of the law officers in June of 1765, the severe criticism of Murray's policy by a lengthy report of the law officers of September 1765 and the comments of Francis Maseres (who later changed his mind) before coming to Canada in 1766. Moreover, Ouellet accepts at its face value Carleton's extravagant rhetoric which shows not only an ignorance of history[85] but a willful blindness to the measures that Murray had already taken for the protection of the Canadians. Even more important he ignores the substantial help already given towards something like the effective establishment of the Church in Canada through the efforts of Murray, Cramahé and Carleton, whose policy was to be continued by Haldimand.

Ouellet also ignores well-known facts on the Canadian scene. Although racial national strife has no doubt been exaggerated, there is much evidence, as one would expect, of some kind of racial-national line between the Canadians and the English. The Canadian and English merchants did not succeed, in spite of a number of efforts in Quebec and Montreal, in agreeing on common petitions to Great Britain on desirable changes in law and government. As for social groupings, the Canadian merchant Baby was a pillar of the official military seigneurial establishment, while the English seigneur Caldwell who, by the economic-social thesis should have voted in Council with his class, offended Carleton by siding on occasion with the merchants. There is no need to exaggerate the occasional Canadian reference to the peril of the "nation" by assuming a full-fledged national self-consciousness, but it is a mistake to go to the other extreme and to suggest that language and religion had no influence on social groups or on political opinions.

Professor Ouellet's work is of very great positive value in its linking of economic developments closely with political events. It has also a negative value which should not be ignored. It is most difficult for a historian opening a new field to correct one error of emphasis without falling into another; to develop fully his new insights without an undue neglect of the work of his predecessors. As so few are without sin in this matter there is the smallest possible temptation to other historians to cast stones.

4. Vincent T. Harlow[86]

Vincent T. Harlow, Beit Professor of the History of the British Empire at Oxford published, in 1952, the first volume of a work on the British Empire which propounded a wholly new thesis. In place of the usual distinction between the first empire of dependent colonies, which ended in 1783, and the second empire of self-governing communities which had its basis in the conquest of 1763, he maintains that the British Empire had always been essentially a trading empire. From the sixteenth century the British had set themselves to break the Spanish monopoly in order that they might enjoy the fruits of the West Indian and South American trade. The American colonies were awkward and not entirely welcome by-products of the failure of this effort. The second empire, also a trading empire, began before 1763 and was characterized not by monopoly but by world-wide expansion of trade centring on free ports and on colonies (in the early period before the mass migrations of the nineteenth century) established in many alien areas not as settlements but chiefly as trading stations and ports of call. The trend to the new imperialism begun before 1763 was accelerated in striking fashion by the almost accidental acquisitions of that year. For the next decade bewildered ministries struggled with or postponed action on unprecedented imperial problems. Harlow sees the important statute of 1774 as a response to a particular situation in North America, which at the same time provided a kind of model for other new and alien areas in the new empire.

The retention of Canada for strategic reasons after the victory of Wolfe precipitated the British into a realm of governmental experience which in its own way was as novel and complex as that other incursion into the unknown occasioned by the battle of Plassey. . . .[87]

Ministers in London had thus stumbled almost unawares into a problem of race relations which was to recur again and again in varying forms during the evolution of an Empire which under the impulsion of industrial development became increasingly multiracial. The fact that a British Administration was required to produce almost simultaneously a system of government for some 20 million Bengalis and about 80,000 French Canadians was symptomatic. These two issues, so different and yet strangely inter-related, caught them at a time when their own political system was at the nadir of confusion. Furthermore the problem of how to incorporate within the imperial system a large "foreign body" in North America was interlocked with incipient revolution in the Thirteen Colonies and the need to rescue a vast continental frontier from anarchy. In this tangled scene, where disunited ministries were groping in search of a policy, are to be found the first tentative experiments in a new form of colonial government which provided an alternative to the standard pattern and by degrees a probationary stage leading on to it.[88]

Harlow discusses the situation in Quebec, the problems of the conflict of laws, the question of religion and government and the sending out of Carleton, who, like Murray, urged special consideration for the Canadians. He mentions the repeated assurances to Carleton, and to Cramahé who succeeded him in the administration in 1770, that the government was about to take action on the problem.

It might seem that such assurances were becoming a stock formula unrelated to practical action, but there is no reason to doubt that successive Ministers were genuinely anxious in spite of the anarchy in domestic politics and growing friction in North America to find a solution for the Canadian problem; but they were in the dark, and perplexed by conflicting opinions. Three different policies were being advocated: quick anglicisation by imposing English legislative and judicial institutions; gradual anglicisation by combining conciliatory measures with the encouragement of immigration from the American Colonies and the weaning of French Canadians from the Roman Catholic faith . . . ; and thirdly Carleton's argument that for the sake of the overriding claims of security French-Canadian privilege and custom must be entrenched.[89]

Harlow does not concede much, if anything, to those who accuse the ministry of indifference to the Canadians, or of neglect, although he does admit that after 1770 the lethargy of North was a delaying factor. He does emphasize that, in addition to the instability of successive ministries, the strong differences of opinion on the complex question of Quebec were an important cause of the long delay in offering a solution.

Even a stable government in time of profound peace might well have hesitated to take the responsibility of imposing its policy in the face of divided counsels from the local experts and a resident Governor. As it was, the Administration of the day was in a state of helpless confusion. In 1769, while the Board of Trade was excogitating a settlement of the Canadian problem, London was in ferment over Wilkes and his thrice repeated election for Middlesex, and a leaderless ministry was faced by mob violence which came near to a revolt. Early in January, 1770, Chatham emerged from seclusion to denounce in passionate and calculated oratory the Ministry which had betrayed his name at home and in America. Chathamites, such as Camden, began shamefacedly to resign, and before the month was out the hapless Grafton threw in his hand. North came in as the King's lieutenant and after a shaky start gathered the support of many moderate men, dismayed by the sudden menace of sweaty nightcaps. The Townsend duties, except on tea, were annulled, and the first blood was shed in the Boston 'massacre'. Although Hillsborough stayed on for two more years as American Secretary, the problems of Quebec remained—under consideration.[90]

Harlow does not think of Carleton as the author or chief inspirer of the Quebec Act. He draws a striking picture of Carleton as "an eighteenth century Curzon . . .," ". . . totally lacking in the art of political management. . . ."[91] He believes that Carleton's contribution in the matter was not the Act itself—"his egoism led him to claim a degree of responsibility for the Quebec Act which was unwarranted"[92]—but an unwarranted expectation of French-Canadian gratitude and support, an expectation with which he deceived himself and the ministry.

Harlow emphasizes that the Act was a sketch to be filled out in the province; that it had reached an advanced stage of planning early in December of 1773; that the Christmas break followed by the alarming news from Boston caused the bill to be set aside until after the penal acts had been passed and then hurried through at the end of the session.

> Thus the interruption caused by these two "Intolerable Acts" held up the Canadian measure, already long delayed, and gave it a legislative juxtaposition which in the existing atmosphere of American suspicion and resentment could not have been more unfortunate.[93]

Harlow regrets the decision not to experiment with an assembly as proposed in 1769. He believes that it might and probably would have ended in deadlock but thinks it was worth trying. By 1773, however, the idea of an assembly had been finally rejected.

> . . . The critical decision had been taken:
> It had been reached by a process of elimination. The series of investigations and reports prepared by officials in Quebec and Ministers and Law Officers in London from 1764 onwards had indicated the emergence of a general consensus that the original guarantee of religious tolerance for an alien society within the empire was not in itself a sufficient means of conciliation. French Canadianism, as expressed in its own social customs, civil law and language, must be respected and adequately recognized. . . . Conciliar government, they concluded, armed with adequate powers but operating under direct imperial control, would be the most effective guarantee of the intended charter of French Canadian privilege; and that in turn would best serve the entrance of British security in a restive North America. The proportionate weight to be attached to these considerations of principle and expediency is less important than the precedent which was established.[94]

Harlow constantly refers to "French Canadianism." It is very difficult in view of the scrappy evidence not to resort to internal evidence to determine the policy of the Act. It is curious, however, that emphasizing as he does a respect for French Canadianism in the Act, Harlow at the same time plays down the influence of Carleton, for only in Carleton's letters is there really clear evidence of this concern.

Harlow, however, does not leave the Act there, and his ultimate conclusion on it may seem slightly inconsistent with this early emphasis on the preservation of French Canadianism. As he points out, Lord Dartmouth, the Colonial Secretary, was officially responsible, and in his view the important decisions of policy were arrived at by Dartmouth and North in consultation. Harlow sees Dartmouth as an ultimate anglicizer whose policy was developed in two distinct but overlapping phases.

The first was the drafting and passing through Parliament of the Act itself. The Act was roughly what Carleton wanted, but Harlow argues, it was strongly influenced by Carleton's most respectable and moderate opponent, William Hey, the Chief Justice of Quebec.

> Hey rejected an elected assembly . . .: but he was a consistent advocate of the proposition that a blending of the two systems of law in such proportions as to satisfy both French and British, combined with a wide religious toleration, could provide a basis for racial harmony and gradual acceptance of assimilation which in due course could be given constitutional expression. This was not the view of Guy Carleton who from 1768 had urged that the only possible way of winning and retaining the loyalty of an ex-enemy community was to guarantee the continuance of its personality. In his view assimilation, if encouraged, would not be with the British system but with American republicanism. Yet it was Hey whose advice as we have seen was increasingly taken by Wedderburn and Dartmouth during the protracted drafting process.[95]

More important, after the Act was passed and Carleton despatched to Quebec, Hey remained in England while Dartmouth prepared the instructions which in his hands "became a gloss upon the Act itself."

> Under the authority of the royal prerogative the Secretary of State took it upon himself to include directives the purpose of which was to conciliate the merchants and win their co-operation, but they did not stem from the terms of the Act. When Carleton received these instructions he found a new legislature was required "to consider well" the desirability of accepting the laws of England as the rule in all cases of personal action covering debts and contracts; and this was followed by a forthright recommendation in favour of adopting

the writ of Habeas Corpus: a fundamental principle of justice in all free governments and an object which the Quebec legislature "ought never to lose sight of it" [sic]. The former was in exact conformity with the terms of Hey's original scheme which, in opposition to Carleton, he had repeated in evidence before the Commons; and the privilege of Habeas Corpus, now so strongly urged, had been stubbornly withheld by North and his colleagues in the Commons in spite of sustained pressure from the Opposition. It is possible that the Ministry had changed their minds after the Act had passed, but there is some evidence to show that Dartmouth had consistently held to the view that it was neither just nor politic to carry the recognition of French-Canadianism so far as to cause legitimate discontent among the English-speaking minority, and it seems more likely that he was now using the weapon of executive authority—after a successful general election and with the assent of North and the King— to restore a balance which had been sacrificed in Parliament for party reasons.[96]

Hey also was required to prepare the draft ordinance for the administration of justice which was sent out to Carleton with Dartmouth's approval to be passed through the Legislative Council. Carleton would naturally have expected that this Act would be prepared in Quebec under his supervision and Harlow sees this as another evidence of the shift of policy from one which Carleton would have approved to that of Carleton's opponent, Chief Justice Hey.

Harlow then sees the Act, along with the instructions, not as a concession extorted by necessity, nor as a charter of liberties, nor as a munificent gift, but as a temporary arrangement, and he sees it as a model for many other such constitutions in the new empire.

. . . in the Commons North emphasized that when a sufficient degree of anglicisation had been achieved the province would be brought into conformity with the rest of the Colonial Empire. A predominantly alien unit was, so to say, to be diverted to a loop line which would eventually join the main constitutional track. The same interpretation of the purpose of "Crown Colony" government was given by Lord Hobart, the Secretary of State in 1804.[97]

Harlow closes his discussion with a wide gesture over the first half century and more of the history of Canada under the British rule.

The acquisition of French Canada thrust Britain into a new field of experience, and not only in North America. The problem of how to incorporate foreign bodies (that is to say, elements that were European but non-British) into the imperial texture was to re-appear twenty years later in many different territories along the ocean-routes which were occupied during a world war for purely strategic reasons. Revolution, war, and political distractions at home bedevilled the experiment of 1774, and further complications arose when the Loyalists and other English-speaking immigrants began to settle in the upper parts of the province. William Grenville devised the Canada Act of 1791 in the hope that the penetrating quality of British institutions would gradually bring about political integration. In that respect he resembled Dartmouth before him and Durham afterwards. Each was working in a different political climate and their methods differed accordingly; but they were alike in their confident reliance on the inherent superiority and power of the British political mould. A century later a similar conviction possessed Milner and Chamberlain. The delusion died hard.[98]

Harlow has gone far beyond any of his predecessors in subjecting the few and scattered materials which bear directly on the passing of the Quebec Act to a minute and scrupulous analysis and he has derived from them a remarkably clear and coherent account of the drafting and the passing of the bill. He has achieved a miracle of imaginative reconstruction. Anxious to elicit British policy and to see it against the background of general imperial responsibility, he deliberately concentrates his attention on London. His comments on Quebec show not much familiarity with French-Canadian society which is over-simplified into "illiterate habitants" and seigneurs, who are presumably literate.

It is a fascinating exercise to follow Harlow's demonstration with the aid of the documents that he uses. This can be done to a certain extent without difficulty, as he draws heavily on the Shortt and Doughty collection. Even when he uses the Dartmouth Papers his sources may be examined in part, as many of these are quoted in footnotes in Shortt and Doughty.

Whoever undertakes the exercise will find Harlow's thesis difficult to disprove. No writer has made a fuller or more fruitful use of the Dartmouth collection. If the thesis cannot be disproved, the reader must still ask himself whether it has been entirely proved. In speaking of the influence of Carleton, the development of Dartmouth's ideas, and the extent to which Chief Justice Hey is involved, Harlow sometimes builds a good deal on slight evidence.[99] But, whether or not he has achieved a true account of the genesis of the Act in London, no one before him has made such an exhaustive use of the material or has produced such a persuasive hypothesis.

NOTES

[1] F. Ouellet, *Histoire Economique et Sociale du Québec, 1760-1850* (Ottawa: Edition Fides, 1966), agrees, in general, with Durham's analysis, although not with his conclusions (p. 438-39).

[2] C. P. Lucas (ed.), *Lord Durham's Report on the Affairs of British North America,* Oxford 1912, Vol. II, pp. 63-65.

[3] *Ibid.,* p. 68.

[4] *Ibid.,* p. 293.

[5] *Ibid.,* pp. 294-95.

[6] *Ibid.,* pp. 295-96.

[7] Francois-Xavier Garneau, *Histoire du Canada depuis sa découverte jusqu'à nos jours* (First published, Quebec 1845). Extracts taken from the edition of 1852. [Editor's translation]

[8] For a remarkably clear picture of the intellectual and political climate in which Garneau wrote see Jacques Monet, S.J., *The Last Cannon Shot* (Toronto: University of Toronto Press, 1970).

[9] Garneau, ed., Quebec 1852, Vol. II, p. 406.

[10] *Ibid.,* pp. 414-15.

[11] William Kingsford, *The History of Canada* (Toronto and London: 1892-   ).

[12] *Ibid.,* Vol. X, p. 533.

[13] *Ibid.,* Vol. V. pp. 146-47.

[14] *Ibid.,* Vol. V, p. 237.

[15] *Ibid.,* Vol. V, pp. 238-39.

[16] *Ibid.,* Vol. V, p. 243.

[17] *Ibid.,* Vol. V, p. 243.

[18] *Ibid.,* Vol. V, pp. 244-45.

[19] Victor Coffin, *The Province of Quebec and the Early American Revolution* (Madison, Wisconsin, The University, 1896).

[20] Goldwin Smith, *Canada and the Canadian Question* (London: Macmillan, 1891), p. 4ff, p. 8ff.

[21] Coffin, pp. v-vi.

[22] *Ibid.,* p. v.

[23] S. & D., p. 670.

[24] *Ibid.,* pp. 660-61.

[25] Coffin, p. 431.

26 *Ibid.,* pp. 431-32.

27 *Ibid.,* p. 433.

28 *Ibid.,* pp. 442-43.

29 See above, p. 81.

30 Coffin, pp. 461-62.

31 *Ibid.,* p. 470.

32 *Ibid.,* pp. 472-73.

33 *Ibid.,* pp, 534, 535-36.

34 Adam Shortt, "The Province of Quebec and the Early American Revolution" [Review article], *Review of Historical Publications Relating to Canada,* Vol. I (Toronto: W. Briggs, 1896).

35 *Ibid.,* pp. 76-77.

36 Martin, Chester. "Professor G. W. Wrong and History in Canada" in Flenley, R. (ed.), *Essays in Canadian History Presented to George MacKenzie Wrong* . . . etc. (Toronto, 1939).

37 John G. Bourinot, *Canada under British Rule* (Toronto: Copp Clark, 1901), pp. 44-45.

38 *Ibid.,* pp. 44-45.

39 S. & D., p. 537, note.

40 Duncan McArthur, "The New Régime," in A. Shortt and A. G. Doughty (eds.) *Canada and its Provinces* (Toronto: Glasgow, Brook Company, 1914).

41 *Ibid.,* Vol. III, pp. 44-45. It will be observed that McArthur and Groulx (page 36) speak of the danger from the American colonies, saying nothing of the fear of an invasion from France, a fear very evident in Carleton's letters. This limited view of the predicament of 1774 is corrected by Burt. Assuming the danger from France to be the greater, one might wonder why Britain did not give at least as much attention to conciliating the Americans as she gave to the Canadians, since the Americans might be a decisive factor in aiding or repelling a French invasion. A more subtle calculation might, however, lead to the conclusion that American aid against French occupation of the St. Lawrence need not be earned, as it would always be offered.

42 *Ibid.,* pp. 46-47

43 *Ibid.,* p. 48.

44 *Ibid.,* p. 49.

45 Thomas Chapais, *Cours d'Histoire du Canada,* Vol. I (Quebec: J.-P. Garneau, 1919-34). [Editor's translation]

46 *Ibid.,* pp. 167-8.

47 Abbé Lionel Groulx, *Vers L'Emancipation* (Montreal: L'Action Française, 1921). [Editor's translation]

48 *Ibid.,* Introduction.

49 *Ibid.,* p. 228.

50 W. P. M. Kennedy, *The Constitution of Canada* (Oxford: Oxford University Press, 1922).

51 He may have been thinking of the so-called "Code Marchand," the French laws governing bankruptcy. There was, in fact, some doubt whether they were valid in Canada.

52 *Ibid.,* pp. 58-59.

53 *Ibid.*, pp. 64-65.

54 *Ibid.*, p. 57, pp. 69-70.

55 *Ibid.*, pp. 68-69, p. 70.

56 *Ibid.*

57 Reginald Coupland, *The Quebec Act* (Oxford: Clarendon Press, 1925).

58 *Ibid.*, pp 127-28.

59 *Ibid.*, pp. 194-96.

60 Chester Martin, *Empire and Commonwealth* (Oxford: Oxford University Press, 1929).

61 *Ibid.*, p. 130.

62 *Ibid.*, pp. 146-47.

63 A. L. Burt, *The Old Province of Quebec* (Minneapolis: University of Minnesota, 1933; Toronto: McClelland & Stewart, 1968). Following page references are to the 1968 edition.

64 *Ibid.*, Vol. I, p. 165.

65 *Ibid.*, pp. 168-69.

66 *Ibid.*, p. 170.

67 *Ibid.*, p. 174.

68 *Ibid.*, p. 180.

69 *Ibid.*, pp. 180-81.

70 C. W. Alvord, *The Mississippi Valley in British Politics* (Cleveland: Arthur H. Clark Co., 1917), Vol. II.

71 *Ibid.*, p. 237ff.

72 S. & D., p. 449 and fn. 3. Shortt and Doughty explain in this footnote that Marriott's idea and the thesis that Alvord has apparently built upon are controverted by the "Papers Relating to the Establishment of Civil Government in the Territories ceded to Britain by the Treaty of 1763" (S. & D., pp. 127-63).

73 Marjorie G. Reid: "The Quebec Fur-Traders and Western Policy 1763-1774," *Canadian Historical Review*, Vol. VI (Toronto: University of Toronto Press, March, 1925).

74 *Ibid.*, pp. 31-32.

75 Louise Kellogg, "A Footnote to the Quebec Act," *Canadian Historical Review*, Vol. XIII (Toronto: University of Toronto Press, June, 1932).

76 *Ibid.*, pp. 153-56.

77 D. G. Creighton, *The Commercial Empire of the St. Lawrence* (New Haven: Yale University Press, 1937); republished in Toronto: Macmillan Company of Canada, 1956, as *The Empire of the St. Lawrence*. Reprinted by permission of the author and The Macmillan Company of Canada Limited.

78 *Ibid.*, pp.74-75.

79 For a full discussion of this matter, see Neatby, *The Administration of Justice under the Quebec Act* (Minneapolis: University of Minnesota Press, 1937), p. 150ff.

80 F. Ouellet, *Histoire Economique et Sociale du Québec 1760-1850* (Montreal: Les Editions Fides, 1966). Reprinted by permission of The Canadian Publishers, McClelland and Stewart Limited, Toronto. [Editor's translation]

81 *Ibid.*, pp. 93-94.

82 S. & D., p. 284.

83 What that policy was is still difficult to determine precisely. There was more justification for Hillsborough's protest than Ouellet admits. Anglicization was contemplated, but so was protection to Canadian law. See S. & D. p. 132, Lords of Trade to Egremont, June 8, 1763, where, in connection with the preservation of Canadian law it is remarked that "for a very long period of time" the number of Canadians must "greatly exceed" English-speaking immigrants. See also R. A. Humphreys: "Lord Shelburne and the Proclamation of 1763" C. H. R. Vol. 49 (1934) p. 241 for evidence on the consistent development of policy during the summer of 1763. See for a discussion of the British viewpoint V. T. Harlow *The Founding of the Second British Empire 1763-1793* Vol. II (1964).

84 William James Smith (ed.), *The Grenville Papers* (London: J. Murray, 1852), Vol. II, p. 476.

85 Carleton borrowed his history (apparently) from Mansfield's statement cited above. Mansfield, in a private letter, used language that he must have known to be extravagant.

86 Vincent T. Harlow: *The Founding of the Second British Empire 1763-1793*, Vol. II (London: Longmans, 1964).

87 *Ibid.*, p. 688.

88 *Ibid.*, p. 668.

89 *Ibid.*, p. 680.

90 *Ibid.*, p. 685.

91 *Ibid.*, p. 706.

92 *Ibid.*, p. 709.

93 *Ibid.*, p. 690.

94 *Ibid.*, p. 687.

95 *Ibid.*, p. 704.

96 *Ibid.*, pp. 710-11.

97 *Ibid.*, p. 713.

98 *Ibid.*, pp. 713-14.

99 There is more evidence, however, for the influence of Hey than Harlow recognizes. Harlow did not have access to the "Dartmouth Originals" in the Public Archives of Canada. One document which, following the views of Shortt and Doughty, he ascribes to Lord Mansfield, was almost certainly the work of Hey. See above, p. 34.

PART 6

The Quebec Act:
Editor's Comment

It is no more than fair that an editor, who, however uneasily, has been sitting in judgment on the work of other historical scholars, should be compelled to expose himself. If the foregoing examples of historical judgments have shown anything, it is that even those few who have dealt thoroughly with the available historical evidence have demonstrated that this evidence is inadequate.

Britain, after 1763, was faced with two problems inextricably entangled with one another, but in their nature distinct. One was the disposition of the Ohio country (where the local war had started in 1754) and the development of just and peaceful relations with the Indian peoples living there. The other was the determination of a mode of government consistent with the general law and practice of the British Empire, for a former French colony. The second problem was undoubtedly difficult, but the main lines of the settlement had already been sketched in the Articles of Capitulation and in the Peace Treaty. All that was needed was to apply the principles agreed on consistently with the general law of the British Empire.

The Treaty was neither explicit nor very generous. It granted freedom of religion to the Canadians "as far as the laws of Great Britain permit." It confirmed the peaceful possession of property only to those Canadians who chose to sell it and leave the country within the space of eighteen months: "So that if they stay," said one commentator, "and claim under the Treaty only, they stay under condition of becoming, by their own free act, *British subjects*; and as such subject to British laws" (S. & D., p. 472). The Articles of Capitulation were more generous. It was argued by some that these could be ignored as superseded by the Treaty. Lord Mansfield, however, was not alone in regarding the Articles of Capitulation as sacred. Advocate General Marriott in making his recommendations for the Quebec Act dealt precisely with the issue: "But the Treaty made with the sovereign state of France . . . does not supersede the Capitulation made with the inhabitants; because I consider capitulations, in the eyes of the law of nations, to be not only

national, but personal compacts and made with the inhabitants themselves, for the consideration of their ceasing their resistance. It is consistent with the honor and interests of this kingdom that they should
be religiously observed . . ." (S. & D., p. 472).

The capitulations then were generally accepted as binding in honour.
These promised the inhabitants, with certain exceptions for religious
orders, complete enjoyment of their property and "the free exercise of
the Catholic, apostolic and Roman religion." It was generally agreed,
as the reports and deliberations of the law officers and officials clearly
show, that the determination of a constitution for Quebec had to be
consistent with these pledges. It is true that the request made to Amherst for a continuation of the custom of Paris under the capitulations
for those who might choose to remain in the country under British rule
was turned aside by his reply, "they become subjects of the King."
Amherst naturally refused to commit himself as to the future laws
which would govern the country should it be retained by Britain. But
common sense as well as legal opinion agreed that the continued peaceful possession of property implied no abrupt or arbitrary change in the
law by which the property was held. Murray and his legal advisors endeavoured to secure this in practice by the ordinance of September 17,
1764; the officials and lawyers and ministers in Britain criticized Murray openly for not giving greater security to Canadian law. The con-
tinuity of the bulk of Canadian civil law in Quebec was never in doubt;
some Canadians complained that the council established by the Quebec
Act could change it at discretion, but this council was under the direct
supervision of the ministry in Great Britain which could and did cause
unacceptable legislation to be disallowed.

It can be said, therefore, that the continuation of much of Canadian
civil law was never seriously threatened. Although the Proclamation of
1763 appeared to contemplate a change, any such intention was re-
pudiated by British ministers, and condemned by Britain's law officers.
The evidence indicates that no legislation by the British Parliament was
needed, and that none would have been passed, but for the apparent
blunder of the Proclamation in promising to confide legislative power
to a hypothetical assembly which in the circumstances could hardly
be summoned.

The obstacle to summoning an assembly was, of course, the religion
of the Canadians. The religious question was more urgent and much
more difficult than the legal one. It might have appeared to call for special legislation, but in fact, as more than one historian has noted, the

Act gave the Roman Catholics very little that they did not already enjoy, and, rigidly applied, it would have restricted rather than extended their liberties.

The Capitulations had promised the free exercise of the Roman Catholic religion in Quebec; the request that the King of France continue to nominate the Bishop was refused, naturally. Unfortunately the question of the Bishop on which Britain remained officially intransigent might have gone far to nullify the concession of "free exercise of worship." Roman Catholics could worship "freely"—in the sense of fully and entirely—only through the ministrations of priests duly ordained by a Bishop duly consecrated under the authority of the Pope. Britain, however, far from recognizing papal authority, was not prepared to countenance in Canada any "Bishop" except the Bishop of the established Church of England. This refusal was completely in accordance with the general practice of civilized nations of western Europe. The Church was an aspect of the state; the Bishop was not only a public official, he was part of the established structure of society of which the King was the head. Authorities in England were quite prepared to tell disgruntled merchants that they must accept Canadian law, as they would that of any other country where they chose to trade, but no one suggested that they must recognize or countenance any but a Bishop of the English church in any British territory.

This delicate problem was solved in a manner typically British. What is important is that it was not settled by the Quebec Act. As far as any Roman Catholic in Quebec knew, it was solved by June 1766 when they welcomed the return from London of Jean-Olivier Briand whom they hailed as their Bishop, and who had been consecrated as such on the authority of papal bulls by three French bishops. He dined at the Governor's table, his authority was supported by the Governor, he dressed like a Bishop, he behaved like one—and he was treated like one, for like all his Canadian predecessors he had trouble with his flock. As for the government, he said, he had rather more freedom of action than he would have had under France.

Officially, Britain knew nothing of this. British officials continued to recommend that a "superintendent" be appointed for the "Romish Church" in Quebec, apparently oblivious of the fact that the church was fully superintended and that ecclesiastical business was going on as usual. This curious situation might be clarified by further research into the operations of the British cabinet, and the relations between ministers, members of the Board of Trade and law officers at this time.

It is quite possible that the arrangements for Briand to go to France for consecration should have been made without leaving a trace on the official records. It is harder to understand how Charles Yorke and William de Grey, discussing benevolently in 1769 what could be done for the Roman Catholics in Quebec, should appear to know nothing of Briand's position and functions in the province. An examination of the relations in the inner circles of government and of the various ecclesiastical schemes proposed for Quebec prior to 1774 might show whether Yorke and de Grey were laboriously registering official unawareness of what was going on in Quebec, or whether they really knew nothing of it.

In fact the Quebec Act recognized a situation already universally accepted. The Act itself was even greeted by the Bishop or "Superintendent" with some alarm. First the proposed oath of allegiance seemed to him inadmissible for Roman Catholics. It was reworded according to his request,[1] but his fears were raised again when he saw in the final form of the Act that the free exercise of religion was "subject to the King's supremacy" according to the Elizabethan Act of Supremacy. It was Carleton who reassured him on this matter. The King, said Carleton, understood the beliefs of his Roman Catholic subjects and he would not interfere with them. "Just keep quiet and believe what you like."[2]

Carleton would have needed to reassure Briand even more about the instructions on religious matters (see above, p. 60) of which he had perhaps heard some rumour.

It may therefore be said that the essential concessions of law and religious freedom could be and were claimed under the capitulations. Apart from a constitutional technicality, the continuation of Canadian law could have been assured without any Parliamentary statute; and the Act, while enforcing, perhaps unecessarily, the tithe, and providing in the instructions a salary for the "Superintendent," provided in the same instructions orders which can only be called harassing and degrading to the Church. If the Quebec Act was a charter for Canadians, like some other charters it may be said only to have confirmed, and with some restrictions, what had already been conceded in practice.

One important exception must be noted to this statement. The granting of civil equality to Canadians by instituting a new oath of office which Roman Catholics were at liberty to take removed a degrading distinction. Even this, however, important as it was, was an application and an extension of the principle enunciated by the law officers in 1765 when they stated that Roman Catholics in colonies abroad ceded to the

King were not subject to the disabilities imposed on Roman Catholics in the United Kingdom. Presumably, therefore, without a statute the Governor might have been authorized to admit Canadians to office on condition of their taking a modified oath.

The main function of the Quebec Act so far as the Canadian community was concerned was to provide for a legislative body other than the promised assembly. Had an assembly been given it could not have been one from which Roman Catholics were excluded, as they must have been, had the usual colonial pattern been followed. The authorities, as was shown by the plan of 1769, were willing to experiment, but by 1773 they had decided that the risks from ignorance, inexperience, and "turbulence" were too great. Not all Canadians were satisfied with this decision. Chartier de Lotbinière complained that the Council was empowered to meddle with Canadian customs which should have been sacred. *Les Vrais Patriotes* (see above, p. 28) wanted an assembly and were willing to pay the price in taxes. Some years later they did get an assembly—and there is good reason for thinking that for all the talk of the seigneurial party about the Quebec Act, most politically-minded Canadians dated their "charter" from 1791 rather than from 1774.

So much for those parts of the Quebec Act that applied specifically to the internal affairs of the conquered French colony. Had the Act, or the British authorities without an Act, done no more than this, there would have been little controversy. Had the adjustments been gradual, as they might have been but for the constitutional doubts about the Council created under the Proclamation, there would almost certainly have been less controversy, less vehement attack from the merchants, less anxious probing of motive and circumstance from English and Canadian nationalists.

What made the Act a centre of the most violent and continued controversy was the geographical, economic and historic connection of the St. Lawrence community with the Ohio country which inspired the boundary clause; and the coincidence in time of the evolution of a policy for the newly-conquered colony with the upsurge of revolutionary activity in the older colonies on the Atlantic coast.

It is impossible to separate the elements in a complex historical situation. It is hopeless to attempt to say what would have happened had one or other of the presumably operative factors been absent. It may, however, be useful, standing a little off from the problem and even from the records, to distinguish the various elements and to notice whether their association with one another is inherent or accidental. To force oneself to look at Quebec out of the context of the Ohio country, and the far North West, and the Atlantic seaboard, is, no doubt, an artificial exercise and therefore dangerous. It has, however, been the purpose of this work to show that historical research *is* dangerous; truth may lie at the bottom of a well both deep and dark.

—H. Neatby

NOTES

1 *Evêques de Québec* (Archives de l'Archevêché de Québec), I: 176. There are, I think, important indications that Briand and Carleton corresponded during the critical years 1770-74, while Carleton was in England. The influence that Briand may have exercised is another of the dark areas of the period, not likely to be cleared up unless some notes or copies by Briand have survived. Carleton's correspondence was destroyed according to his own wishes.

2 *Rapport de l'Archiviste de la Province de Québec* (*RAPQ*) 1929-30, p. 109; quoted in Helen G. Manning, *The Revolt of French Canada 1800-1836* (Toronto: The Macmillan Company of Canada, 1962), pp. 32-33.